HALLOWED BE THY NAME

WARREN HENDERSON

HALLOWED BE THY NAME

Revering CHRIST in a Casual World

All Scripture quotations from the King James
Version of the Bible unless otherwise noted.

Hallowed Be Thy Name
By Warren Henderson
Copyright © 2006

Published by Gospel Folio Press
304 Killaly Street West
Port Colborne, ON, L3K 6A6, Canada

Cover Design by Rachel Brooks

ISBN 1-897117-45-0

ORDERING INFORMATION:
Gospel Folio Press
Phone 1-905-835-9166
E-mail: order@gospelfolio.com

Printed in the United States of America

Table of Contents

<u>Acknowledgements</u>

The author is indebted to all those who contributed to the publishing of *Hallowed Be Thy Name*. I praise the Lord and thank Him for each of you. Much gratitude to the following brethren for their editorial contributions: Randy Amos, Mike Attwood, John Bjorlie, David Dunlap, Steve Hulshizer, Jabe Nicholson, and Jack Spender. Special thanks also to Jane Biberstein for general editing and David Lindstrom for proofreading assistance.

Preface

When friends or loved ones perform well at a piano recital or in some sporting event or obtain some academic achievement, we offer them congratulations. If we truly care, recognizing accomplishments and rendering admiration is almost effortless. Similarly, our disgust is prompted when others engage in immoral conduct or unethical business practices. The acute aspects of what is right and wrong, honourable and dishonourable, wise and foolish, are for the most part apparent to God's people. However, it is those familiar affairs of life, matters which seem acceptable to us, more on the basis of familiarity, than merit, that require more diligence in distinguishing error. Indeed, our flesh has a natural propensity to not question what is customary in life, even if it may be unapproved by God – we love the *status quo*.

The expression "you can't see the forest because of the trees" has a variety of applications, but we tend to think of others as being short-sighted, ignorant or proud before personally applying the term. Of particular exercise in the writing of this book is for the reader to step back from the religious jargon, spiritual terminology and Church traditions of the day and validate whether the biblical forest is still there. Is it possible that some of our common rote, our familiar terminology, and our generational traditions affront God and stifle the working of the Holy Spirit in our lives?

Twice, while speaking through the prophet Haggai, the Lord told the children of Israel to *"Consider your ways" (Hag. 1:5, 7).* May the following study cause the reader, as it did me, to consider *your ways.* We don't want to be engaging in any activity or speech which dethrones the Lord and exalts men. Occasionally, in a Bible study or a counseling session, I will hear someone say, "I never thought about that before." Well, it's time to think! In matters of revealed truth our ignorance is not bliss; in fact, whether willful or not, it insults God (e.g. 2 Kings 22:13).

Is scriptural terminology important? Does wrong terminology tend to lead to erroneous Church practices? Do I ignorantly show disdain for the Lord's name by the way in which I address Him or speak of Him to others? What is the sin of blasphemy? Can a Christian blaspheme God today? Do I show a lack of reverence for the Lord through vain religious practices and celebrations? These are some of the questions this book examines in detail. Our speech and behaviour reflect our heart's adoration for the Lord Jesus and, thus, directly affect our testimony of Him to the world. May God bestow on us grace to *"buy the truth, and sell it not"* (Prov. 23:23), and may each one be subject to the *"good, and acceptable, and perfect, will of God"* (Rom. 12:2).

What's in a Name?

The Lord Jesus regularly – often in the pre-dawn hours of the day – enjoyed private and personal communion with His Father. The disciples had witnessed the Lord's inspiring prayer-life, and they, too, desired a meaningful experience with God. They earnestly petitioned the Saviour, *"Lord, teach us to pray"* (Luke 11:1). The Lord did just that, but not by teaching them a prayer to be recycled – He taught them in what "manner" to pray (i.e. how to pray, Matt. 6:9). The Lord commenced the instruction by addressing His Father in this way: *"Our Father which art in heaven, hallowed be Thy name"* (Matt. 6:9). God, His name, and His dwelling place transcend all that is common and earthly. God is Holy; He is separate from all else! All that is associated with Him, including His name, should be revered.

In the Old Testament, a great significance is attached to personal names, for a name reveals not just the identity of a person but also their features and character. Jacob lived up to his name, meaning "supplanter" – a trickster and schemer. Esau's name related to the hairy feature of his body at birth. The prophetic rendering of divine names throughout the Old Testament had substantial importance to God's people for God was revealing Himself in relationship to them. A note in the *Cambridge Annotated Study Bible* more fully expounds this point:

> The name of God holds an important key to understanding the doctrine of God and the doctrine of revelation. The name of

God is a personal disclosure and reveals His relationship with His people. His name is known only because He chooses to make it known. To the Hebrew mind, God was both hidden and revealed, transcendent and immanent. Even though He was mysterious, lofty, and unapproachable, He bridged the gap with humankind by revealing His name.

The truth of God's character is focused in His name. The divine name reveals God's power, authority, and holiness. This accounts for Israel's great reverence for God's name. The Ten Commandments prohibited the violation of God's name (Ex. 20:7; Deut. 5:11). Prophets spoke with authority when they uttered God's name. Oaths taken in God's name were considered binding, and battles fought in the name of God were victorious. Other nations would fear Israel, not because it was a mighty nation, but because it rallied under the Lord's name.[1]

Charles Haddon Spurgeon said:

The proper study of a Christian is the Godhead. The highest science, the loftiest speculation, the mightiest philosophy which can ever engage the attention of a child of God is the name, the person, the work, the doings, and the existence of the great God whom he calls his Father.[2]

Certainly the Lord Jesus was about the business of declaring God's great name before men. The evening before His crucifixion, while speaking to His Father, He said *"I have manifested Thy name unto the men..."* (John 17:6). Knowing God's personal names is really a prerequisite of knowing God Himself. To fabricate God through mental images, humanly ascribed names and earthly forms is nothing less than pernicious idolatry. To approach God by any other name or way than what He has revealed in Scripture is vain religion. May we know and esteem God's various names, for in them He beckons us to draw near and know Him more deeply. On this point Nikita Ivanovich Panin wrote:

> The world we inhabit must have had an origin; that origin must have consisted in a cause; that cause must have been intelligent; that intelligence must have been supreme; and that supreme, which always was and is supreme, we know by the name of God.[3]

Dear reader, to what degree do you know and appreciate the names of God? You will not value what you do not understand, nor will you sacrifice for what you do not appreciate. Some of the most astonishing scriptural revelations of God's holy character and divine essence are found in His names. Unfortunately, the Church often neglects the most crucial studies in preference of doing something for God. But the whole focus of discipleship is summed up in "being," not "doing." The Lord Jesus did not say to His followers, "you cannot *become* My disciples…"; He stressed "you cannot *be* my disciples …." Discipleship is a life-long pursuit of Christ; it is not something you suddenly arrive at one morning. A true disciple of Christ is compelled to learn of Christ (Matt. 11:29) and to be like Christ (Matt. 10:25). Before we can contemplate honouring the Lord and reverencing His names, we must first know Him and the meaning of His names.

Names for God in the Old Testament

As numerous books have been written concerning the different names of God; the following list serves only as a brief reminder of the more frequently used names of God in the Old Testament.

Yahweh

Yahweh is translated as "Jehovah" in some English versions of the Bible, but normally it is rendered as "the Lord" or "O Lord." *Yahweh* is rendered from the Hebrew tetragrammaton YHWH and represents God's personal name as revealed to His covenant people the Jews. When reading the Hebrew text many Jewish scholars substitute "Adonai" for YHWH to avoid pronouncing the sacred name of God. Yahweh is found 6,828 times in the Old Testament and most likely relates to the verb "to be;" for Yahweh is the self-existent one. In Exodus 3:14, the Lord declares, "I AM THAT I AM." As there are no vowels in the Hebrew written language, no one is quite sure how God's covenant name is to be pronounced.

Elohim

Elohim is normally rendered "God" in the English translations and emphasizes God's transcendence and majesty: God is preeminent above all creation and certainly above all humanly contrived deities. *Elohim* is the plural form of *eloah*. The Hebrew language has singular, dual and plural forms. *Elohim* is the form used to express an association of three or more and, thus, reflects the triune nature of God revealed from the whole of Scripture.

Adonai

The root meaning of *Adonai* is "lord" or "master." *Adonai* is normally translated "Lord" in English Bibles. Of the 449 times *Adonai* occurs in the Old Testament, it is used in conjunction with *Yahweh* 315 times. *Nelson's Expository Dictionary* notes:

> *Adhon* emphasizes the servant-master relationship (cf. Gen. 24:9) and thus suggests God's authority as Master;

One who is sovereign in His rule and has absolute authority (cf. Ps. 8:1; Hos. 12:14). *Adonai* should probably be understood as meaning "Lord of all" or "Lord par excellence" (cf. Deut. 10:17; Josh. 3:11).[4]

Eloah

Eloah is a generic name for deity in the Old Testament (God). It is interesting that it is only found fifty-seven times in the Old Testament as compared to its plural form *Elohim*, which is found some 2600 times. *Elohim* more accurately attests to a triune nature of God; His *plural unity*. It is noted that the majority of *Eloah* references are located in the book of Job.

El

El, is the common Semitic name for deity (god) in ancient Eastern cultures and is found 245 times in the Old Testament. *El* simply refers to a moral superior. It does not always refer to true divinity; *El* may be translated "god," "man," "angel," etc. *El* is often compounded with other names of God in the Old Testament.

Besides the frequently used names and references to God just mentioned, a number of compound forms of the name of God involving the names El (or Elohim) and Yahweh may be found throughout Scripture. *The Moody Handbook of Theology* lists the following compound names of God:

> *El Shaddai.* Translated "God Almighty," it perhaps relates to the word *mountain* and suggests the power or strength of God. By this name God is also seen as a covenant-keeping God (Gen. 17:1; cf. vv. 1–8 where the covenant is reiterated).

7

El Elyon. Translated "God Most High," it emphasizes the supremacy of God. He is above all so-called gods (cf. Gen. 14:18–22). Melchizedek recognized Him as "God Most High" inasmuch as He is possessor of heaven and earth (v. 19).

El Olam. Translated the "Everlasting God," it stresses the unchanging character of God (Gen. 21:33; Isa. 40:28).

Other Names. There are other compound terms that are sometimes mentioned as names of God, but they may simply be descriptions of God:

Yahweh-jireh, "The LORD Will Provide" (Gen. 22:14)
Yahweh-Nissi , "The LORD Our Banner" (Ex. 17:15)
Yahweh-Shalom, "The LORD is Peace" (Judg. 6:24)
Yahweh-Sabbaoth, "The LORD of Hosts" (1 Sam. 1:3)
Yahweh-Maccaddeshcem, "The LORD Thy Sanctifier" (Ex. 31:13)
Yahweh-Tsidkenu, "The LORD Our Righteousness" (Jer. 23:6)[5]

Sometimes the Old Testament writers combined several different names of God in a particular passage to confirm the awesome nature or workings of God. Alluding to the security of God's presence in Psalm 91, the psalmist used the four chief names for God in the first two verses. Each name corroborates the manifold power of God as our divine refuge and strength:

*He that dwelleth in the secret place of the **Most High** (El Elyon) shall abide under the shadow of the **Almighty** (Shaddai). I will say of the **LORD** (Jehovah), He is my refuge and my fortress: my **God** (Elohim); in Him will I trust"* (Ps. 91:1-2).

Names for God in the New Testament

The names of God applied in the New Testament reflect Old Testament terminology and Jewish tradition, but as related to a Greek-speaking culture. The following are New Testament names of God; some refer specifically to the Lord Jesus Christ:

God
Derived from the Greek word *theos*, this is the most common word for God in the New Testament (found 1,318 times). In the Septuagint (the Greek version of the Old Testament) *theos* is used over 4000 times in reference to God and is the prime equivalent of the Hebrew word *elohim*.

Lord
Just as the Greek word *theos* is the prime equivalent of *elohim* in the Old Testament, the Greek word *kyrios*, translated "Lord," is most often equated to God's personal name *Yahweh* in the Septuagint. Not only does *kyrios* denote deity, it conveys the message of mastership: God is Creator, Owner and Ruler over all Creation – He is to be obeyed. Interestingly, the vast majority of the 719 occurrences of *kyrios* in the New Testament refer to Jesus Christ (nearly all references are after His exaltation). Thus, the two most common Old Testament names for deity, "God" and "Lord," are used in the New Testament not only in reference to God but also in reference to the Lord Jesus. Thus, He as God is called Lord in the same way His Father is Lord God.

Father
Most of the New Testament names for God are found in one form or another in the Old Testament, but one

significant name – "Father" – is not, at least not in the same familiarity. A few passages express the Fatherly *position* of God, but not relational *intimacy of sonship*: *"A Father of the fatherless, a judge [a defender] of the widows, is God in His holy habitation"* (Ps. 68:5). *"If then I am the Father, where is My honor? And if I am a Master, where is my reverence? Says the Lord of hosts"* (Mal. 1:6, NKJV). *"Have we not all one Father? Hath not one God created us?"* (Mal. 2:10). Old Testament saints did not refer in a familiar sense to God as "Father." This is strictly a New Testament dynamic obtained through the gospel of Jesus Christ. The Lord said on resurrection day, while speaking to Mary Magdalene, *"I ascend unto My Father, and your Father; and to My God, and your God"* (John 20:17). In the Old Testament we read of the "children of Israel" and the "people of God," but it is not until the New Testament that the intimate term "children of God" is found.

The God of the Fathers
P. J. Achtemeier comments:

> This significant Old Testament title for God, as well as the more particular phrase of the same meaning, 'the God of Abraham, Isaac, and Jacob,' is found in the New Testament only in two Gospels (Mark 12:26; Matt. 22:32) and in the book of Acts. As in the Old Testament, it emphasizes the continuity of Israel and the church's faith, that the God of present experience is the same as the God revealed to the ancient patriarchs.[6]

The Almighty

P. J. Achtemeier again helps to explain the meaning of this name for God:

> The Septuagint had translated two of the Hebrew expressions for God in the Old Testament, which probably meant 'God, the one of the mountains' (RSV: 'God Almighty') and 'Yahweh of Hosts,' with the more philosophical and formal *pantokratōr* (Greek, 'Almighty') ....[It] is found only in 2 Cor. 6:18 and nine times in Revelation, mostly in self-designations of God or in ascriptions of praise in a liturgical context.[7]

The Alpha and Omega

Alpha is the first letter in the Greek alphabet, and Omega is the last. Thus, the reference to these two letters figuratively represent God as the Beginning and the End. He is eternal, the source of life, the creator of all creation and, thus, the only true God. In the New Testament, only the book of Revelation uses this name for God (Rev. 1:8; 21:6), and John clearly refers to the Lord Jesus as the Alpha and Omega (Rev. 1:8; Rev. 22:13). The expression Alpha and Omega is similar to our English expression "from A to Z" which means "the entire thing – the whole alphabet." As God's Alphabet Christ is God's entire communication. He is "the Word of God." *"Beginning at Moses and all the prophets, He expounded unto them, in all the Scriptures, the things concerning Himself"* (Luke 24:27).

The Holy One

This is a title for God found in the Old Testament, but used only once in the New Testament to refer explicitly to God (Rev. 16:5, NASV). However, at least three times in the New Testament this name of God is used in addressing the Lord Jesus (Mark 1:24; Luke 4:34; John 6:69, NASV).

To Contemplate the Names of God

What marvelous revelation and comfort are found in the names of God (that is for those who choose to honour Him)! In the first verse of Scripture, God identifies Himself as *Elohim* – a name that links Him with creation. The basic root *El*, which means "mighty and strong," is then frequently reused and combined with other names to broaden our understanding of God's character and nature. Before departing Genesis 2, we are introduced to the "Lord God" – *Jehovah Elohim*. As stated previously, *Jehovah* is the covenant name of God which intimately connects Him to His people.

At Horeb, while investigating a bush that was not consumed by fire, Moses was introduced to His Creator; God told Moses: *"I AM that I AM"* (Ex. 3:14). Moses hid his face from God in reverential fear, and God then instructed Moses to remove his shoes for he was standing upon holy ground (He was in the very presence of God.). Shoes represent the works of our hands and our *will* (With shoes upon our feet, we venture where *we will*.). Moses learned that he could not approach I AM, the self-existing and unchanging God of the universe, through doing good works and that only God's will for his life mattered – a holy life is a consecrated life centered in the will of God. All life is in I AM, and apart from Him, there is no spiritual life or holy living.

The Lord Jesus repeatedly stated that He was God, though He had become flesh (John 1:14), by directly applying the "I AM" affirmations of the Old Testament to Himself. When speaking of Jesus Christ, the writers of the New Testament confirm the same: *"All things were made by Him; and without Him was not anything made that was made"* (John 1:3). *"By Him were all things created ... He is before all things, and by Him all things consist"* (Col. 1:16-17). Many of the Old Testament names for God are applied directly to the Lord Jesus, thus affirming His deity and also demonstrating the unique importance of each of God's names in representation of His overall essence.

Dear reader, if you found this chapter a little slow or uninteresting, please recall that God chose to reveal Himself to us through His unique names. To encourage the reader's personal study of this important subject Appendix A contains over four hundred names, titles and references to Christ found throughout Scripture. Because God's names are so intimately tied with His character, each is to be honoured and revered, not flippantly used. Harry A. Ironside punctuates this point:

> God has said, *"By those who come near Me, I must be regarded as holy"* (Lev.10:3). *"Holy and awesome is His name" (Ps. 111:9).* As we approach Him we should do so in reverence and godly fear (Heb. 12:28). The name of God tells of what and who He is. It speaks of the divine character. Believers take His name upon them when they are identified with Him by profession of their faith in Him. The careless use of divine names and titles betrays a grossly irreverent state of mind, and is itself a grave sin against Him who is Creator of all men and Father of all who believe. We are called to *"walk worthy of God"* (1 Thess. 2:12) because He is our Father and we are His children. Irreverence on the part of those who profess this high and holy calling is most deplorable and is, in effect, to take the name of the Lord our God in vain. To profess to love God and yet to dishonour Him by a godless and worldly life is to take that holy name in vain just as much as to be guilty of the irreverent use of holy expressions. In all our ways we are called upon to sanctify the Lord and thus to honour His holy name.[8]

God's names are powerful, for in them we learn of His character, His essence, His divine attributes, His authority and His holiness. When someone uses God's name vainly or associates it with common things, He is insulted. To honour God, one must reverence His name. The Psalmist wrote: *"He sent redemption unto His people: He hath commanded His covenant for ever: **Holy and Reverend is His name"*** (Ps. 111:9). The prophet Isaiah declared: *"For thus saith the high and lofty **One that inhabiteth eternity, whose name is Holy**; I dwell in the high and holy place, with him also that is of a contrite and humble spirit, to revive the spirit of the humble, and to revive the heart of the contrite ones"* (Isa. 57:15). One conclusion in the matter of God's name is alone possible: *"Praise be to the name of God for ever and ever; wisdom and power are His"* (Dan. 2:20, NIV).

> Only to sit and think of God,
> Oh what a joy it is!
> To think the thought, to breathe the name –
> Earth has no higher bliss.

> — Frederick William Faber

The Third Commandment

Did you know that the image and name of Smokey Bear are protected by U.S. federal law?[1] It's true; in 1952, an Act of Congress took Smokey out of the public domain and put him under the control of the Secretary of Agriculture. The imaginary bear who has labored to prevent forest fires for over sixty years is to be esteemed – no inappropriate use of his name or image is allowed by law. However, to speak the Lord's name in vain, which violates the third of the Ten Commandments is legalized "free speech." Civil law allows the slandering of God's name, but not Smokey's!

Paul warned Timothy that in the latter days *"men shall be lovers of their own selves, covetous, boasters, proud, blasphemers... (2 Tim 3:2).* Highly esteeming oneself directly brings God low in our minds, and this will be a characteristic trait of the final days of the Church Age – men will blaspheme God and use His name in vain. The days of which Paul spoke have arrived. Not only is it lawful to use the Lord's name in vain, but it is increasingly fashionable to do so in many social circles. Yet, this violation was not always the norm; in fact our nation's forefathers esteemed the name of the Lord and drafted laws to guard against using it unworthily.

In the early years of our nation's history, civil law directly affirmed the Third Commandment: *"Thou shalt not take the name of the Lord thy God in vain; for the Lord will not hold him guiltless that taketh His name in vain"* (Ex. 20:7). The following two court cases serve as historical examples:

> **Massachusetts Supreme Court** (1838), heard the case of *Commonwealth v. Abner Kneeland,* 37 Mass. (20 Pick) 206, 216–217 1838, which involved a Universalist who claimed the right of "freedom of the press" as a defense for publishing libelous and defamatory remarks about Christianity and God. The Court delivered its decision, stating that "freedom of the press" was not a license to print without restraint, otherwise:
>
> > According to the argument ... every act, however injurious or criminal, which can be committed by the use of language may be committed ... if such language is printed. Not only therefore would the article in question become a general license for scandal, calumny and falsehood against individuals, institutions and governments, in the form of publication ... but all incitation to treason, assassination, and all other crimes, however atrocious, if conveyed in printed language, would be dispunishable.

The statute, on which the case was based is quite long, but the central issue was that a violator must be punished (by incarceration and/or fines).

> "If any person shall willfully blaspheme the holy name of God, by denying, cursing, or contumeliously reproaching God, His creation, government, or final judging of the world..."[2]

Connecticut General Court, Code of the (1650), in the Capital Laws Section of the Code, stated offenses and their punishments:

1. If any man after legal conviction shall have or worship any other God but the Lord God, he shall be put to death. Deut. 13:6, 17:2; Ex. 22:20.

2. If any man or woman be a witch, that is, has or consults with a familiar spirit, they shall be put to death. Ex. 22:18; Lev. 20:27; Deut. 18:10, 11.

3. If any person shall blaspheme the Name of God the Father, Son or Holy Ghost with direct, express, presumptuous, or high-handed blasphemy, or shall curse in the like manner, he shall be put to death. Lev. 24:15, 16. [Articles 4 and 5 are not listed.]

6. If any man or woman shall lie with any beast or brute creature, by carnal copulation, they shall surely be put to death, and the beast shall be slain and buried. Lev. 20:15, 16.

7. If any man lies with mankind as he lies with a woman, both of them have committed abomination, they both shall surely be put to death. Lev. 20:13.[3]

Notice the order in which the laws are written. The worship of other gods, occult practices, or the dishonouring of God through speech is addressed first, then the carnal perversions that defile men are mentioned afterwards. The recompense for each violation carries the full strength of the Levitical law – the death penalty. How serious of an offense it is to God to use His name vainly! Our nation's forefathers fully understood the grievous nature of the sin, but over time our reverence for God and His name have waned.

Charles Cotesworth Pinckney had many political achievements; he was one of the signers of the U.S. Constitution, was a delegate to the Constitutional Convention, and assisted in the writing of the Constitution of the State of South Carolina. Pinckney once said, "Blasphemy against the Almighty is denying His being or providence, or uttering contumelious reproaches on our Saviour Christ. It is punished, at common law by fine and imprisonment, for Christianity is part of the laws of the land."[4]

By the twentieth century, using the Lord's name vainly had become more acceptable in public, but in general the entertainment industry avoided the practice until the mid-twentieth century. Carol Norris Greene recounts how the American motion picture studios in Hollywood changed their position on the matter:

> In 1922, when the public feared that the immorality thought to be widespread in Hollywood might appear on screen, the Motion Picture Producers and Distributors of America, headed by Will H. Hays, established a film review board to develop a code of conduct for Hollywood producers. In the board's Motion Picture Production Code of 1930 – popularly known as the *Hays Code* – Article "V. Profanity" stated: "Pointed profanity (this includes the words 'God,' 'Lord,' 'Jesus,' 'Christ' – unless used reverently – 'hell,' 'S.O.B.,' 'damn,' 'Gawd') or every other profane or vulgar expression however used, is forbidden." Imagine that: The blasphemous use of the Lord's name was so prevalent even then that it had to be listed in a code of restrictions!

> In 1966, the Hays Code was abandoned by filmmakers who did not wish to be governed by its bans on sexuality and violence. It was succeeded by the Motion Picture Code and Rating Program that we are familiar with today, which purports to offer guidance for parents, not filmmakers.[5]

Can you imagine the wide-sweeping effect of enforcing the past Connecticut and Massachusetts' laws concerning blasphemy today? How many movies, advertisements, books, magazines, newspapers, Internet chat-rooms, billboards, and radio and television programs would have to be terminated because of inappropriate use of God's name. The answer is, most! Carnal man bemoans, "You're violating my rights," but God declares, "You're violating My name!" Scripture declares, *"The Lord will not hold him guiltless that taketh His name in vain"* (Ex. 20:7). Why does God take so seriously the use of His name? Charles Hodge explains:

> To call on the name of the Lord, and to call on God, are synonymous forms of expression. As names are intended to distinguish one person or thing from another, anything distinguishing or characteristic may be included under the term. The name of God, therefore, includes everything by which He makes Himself known. This commandment [the third of the Ten Commandments], therefore, forbids all irreverence towards God; not only the highest act of irreverence in calling on Him to bear witness to a falsehood, but also all irreverent use of His name; all careless, unnecessary reference to Him, or His attributes; all indecorous conduct in His worship; and in short, every indication of the want of that fear, reverence, and awe due to a Being infinite in all His perfections, on whom we are absolutely dependent, and to whom we are accountable for our character and conduct.[6]

Practically speaking, what does obedience to the third of the Ten Commandments entail? How can I know if I am breaking this commandment? Charles Hodge again clarifies the matter for us:

> The third commandment, therefore, specially forbids not only perjury, but also all profane, or unnecessary oaths, all careless appeals to God, and all irreverent use of His name. All literature,

19

whether profane or Christian, shows how strong is the tendency in human nature to introduce the name of God even on the most trivial occasions. Not only are those formulas, such as Adieu, Good-bye or God be with you, and God forbid, which may have had a pious origin, constantly used without any recognition of their true import, but even persons professing to fear God often allow themselves to use His name as a mere expression of surprise. God is everywhere present. He hears all we say. He is worthy of the highest reverence; and He will not hold him guiltless who on any occasion uses His name irreverently. [7]

The Old Testament contains several examples of individuals who blasphemed the Lord's name and the consequences they suffered for so doing. One of the most intriguing narratives involving blasphemy relates the occasion where a non-Jewish man, and thus unfamiliar with the Law, is given the death penalty for blaspheming the name of the Lord (Lev. 24:10-23). Leviticus is the worship manual of Israel – it provided the means for God's people to draw near to God through animal sacrifices (i.e. through the shedding and applying of blood). At first glance, one might wonder why the Levitical instruction was interrupted in order to record the fact that a blasphemer was judged, but the event illustrated God's holiness and, therefore, is not an interruption. God was to be reverenced in the land, and not even "strangers" were to blaspheme the name of the God of Israel. Warren Wiersbe explains:

The basis for obedience to the law is the fear of the Lord, and people who blaspheme His holy name have no fear of God in their hearts. Every Jew knew the third commandment: *"You shall not take the name of the Lord your God in vain, for the Lord will not hold him guiltless who takes His name in vain"* (Ex. 20:7, NKJV). So fearful were the Jews of breaking this commandment that they substituted the name "Adonai" for "Jehovah" when they read the Scriptures, thus never speaking God's name at all. To respect a name is to respect the person who bears that name, and our highest respect belongs to the Lord.[8]

The practice of the orthodox Jews of not saying Yahweh or Jehovah reflects their fear of God and reverence for His name, and unfortunately their ignorance of Him. As in the days of Esther, the Jewish nation is out of touch with God; their spiritual state precludes them from knowing God personally and intimately. Authority without relationship promotes fear, so today, the Jews are abiding *"many days without king or prince, without sacrifice, or sacred pillar, without ephod or teraphim"* (Hosea 3:4). Though they know not God personally, they do revere His name.

Our nation's forefathers also reverenced the name of the Lord. Civil statutes were commonly founded upon God's law; consequently, the name of the Lord was protected from slander and evil speaking. Much has changed, but the worst of the matter is that much of the "professing" Church is engaged in blaspheming the name of the Lord, and *"the Lord will not hold him guiltless who takes His name in vain."*

Blasphemy

What is blasphemy? Can this grievous sin be committed today? Can a Christian blaspheme God? These are important questions, and the Word of God provides answers to each. First, let us examine the meaning of blasphemy.

In the New Testament, the word "blasphemy" appears in both a noun form *blasphemia*, occurring nineteen times, and in a verb form *blasphemeo*, found thirty-five times. *Blasphemia* is translated "blasphemy," "evil speaking," and "railing." It denotes "slander or speech injurious to another's good name (Matt. 12:31) or impious speech disdaining divine majesty (Matt. 26:65)." *Blasphemeo* is rendered "blaspheme" (-er, -mously, -my), "defame," "rail on," "revile," "speak evil." It is the act of "speaking reproachfully, to rail at, or to revile (especially against God)."

It is hard to fathom a day that man has blasphemed his Creator more than that dark day when mankind mocked, spit upon, beat, scourged, and then nailed Him to a cross. Human insurrection surged at the very juncture in time when the precious Saviour suffered on humanity's behalf. During this event Scripture applies the Greek *blasphemeo* in the following insults:

> *And the men that held Jesus mocked Him, and smote Him. And when they had blindfolded Him, they struck Him on the face, and asked Him, saying, Prophesy, who is it that smote Thee? And many other things **blasphemously** spake they against Him* (Luke 22:63-65).

*And they that passed by **railed on** Him, wagging their heads, and saying, Ah, Thou that destroyest the temple, and buildest it in three days Save Thyself, and come down from the cross. Likewise also the chief priests, mocking, said among themselves with the scribes, He saved others; Himself he cannot save* (Mark 15:29-31).

*And one of the malefactors which were hanged **railed on** Him, saying, If Thou be Christ, save Thyself and us* (Luke 23:39).

When an individual rails, slanders or speaks evil against God to cause injury, harm or offense, that individual has blasphemed God. Specifically applied, the sin of blasphemy involves showing disdain or a lack of reverence for God or for what He deems as sacred (Matt. 26:65), or attributing divine characteristics to something or someone other than God. (The Jews accused Jesus of doing this, see Mark 14:64.) The psalmist sums the matter up concisely – only fools blaspheme the name of God! *"Remember this, that the enemy hath reproached, O Lord, and that the foolish people have blasphemed Thy name"* (Ps. 74:18).

This psalm contains the plea of God's people for the Lord's help and restoration and for His judgement upon their adversaries who pompously blaspheme the name of the Lord. *"O God, how long shall the adversary reproach? Shall the enemy blaspheme Thy name forever?* (Ps. 74:10). Matthew Henry provides a splendid devotional thought in conjunction with honouring the name of God:

As nothing grieves the saints more than to hear God's name blasphemed, so nothing encourages them more to hope that God will appear against their enemies than when they have arrived at such a pitch of wickedness as to reproach God Himself; this fills the measure of their sins apace and hastens their ruin. The psalmist insists much upon this: "We dare not answer their reproaches; Lord, do Thou answer them. Remember that

24

the *foolish people have blasphemed Thy name* and that still *the foolish man reproaches Thee daily."'* Observe the character of those that reproach God; they are foolish. As atheism is folly (Ps. 14:1), profaneness and blasphemy are no less so.[1]

The foolishness of man is never more obvious than when he maligns his Creator. The "mystery of iniquity" will run its due course. Man scoffed at God's impending judgement during the days of Noah; man blasphemed God as Paul preached the gospel message (Acts 26:11), and blasphemy of God will be unchecked during the future Tribulation Period for the anti-Christ will speak great blasphemies (Rev. 13:6).

As stated earlier, the increase of mankind's blasphemy against God is a sign of the end of the Church Age (2 Tim. 3:1-2). It is my opinion that we are in the last days of the Church Age. Perhaps the anti-Christ is alive on planet earth at this present hour. If so, the hour of horrific holocaust of life and the hour of unmatched insult to God is at hand.

A century ago, one could be fined and publicly ostracized for using the Lord's name in vain, but today, as "the man of sin" prepares to rule the world, the sin of blasphemy – the folly of man – is rampant. The message for the Christian, however, is this: We need not take part in the desecration of God's name – for hallowed is His name! For many Christians, a relearning of righteous speech patterns and proper conduct to honour God's name are required. That the unsaved will lack reverence for the Lord's name is somewhat understandable, but why do Christians debase God's name in speech or in conduct, often unconscious of doing so?

You may be thinking to yourself, "I don't blaspheme the Lord or show disrespect to His name!" I implore you to read on, for in one form or another, we often unconsciously demean God's name. This problem seems to have been present even in

25

the early church, for Paul exhorts believers more than once to put away all evil speech and blasphemies (Eph. 4:31, Col. 3:8).

Because Hymenaeus and Alexander had abandoned a good conscience and shipwrecked their faith, Paul committed them to the Lord in prayer, and unto Satan for buffeting. The end goal was *"that they may learn not to blaspheme"* (1 Tim. 1:20). William MacDonald comments on this passage:

> In the New Testament, *blaspheme* does not always mean to speak evil of God.... It might be used to describe the lives of these men as well as the words of their lips. By making shipwreck of the faith, they had undoubtedly caused others to speak evil of the way of truth, and thus their lives were living blasphemies.[2]

The Bible contains examples of individuals who blasphemed God and reveals that this sin will continue through the Church Age and into the Tribulation Period. God's exhortation to all believers is *"Be ye holy for I AM holy"* (1 Pet. 1:16). Not only are Christians not to speak blasphemy, but they must strive not to live blasphemy either (Jas. 2:7). God's will for the believer is that he or she should refrain from doing sin, and that he or she indeed practice a sin-free life altogether (1 Jn. 2:1). However, on this side of glory, sinless perfection is a pursuit, not a reality – thank God our salvation is not based on our doings, but upon His grace. And, praise be to God, our new nature received at conversion cannot sin (1 Jn. 3:9). Let us all pursue holiness, for in holiness we find not the inability to sin, but the ability not to sin.

The Unpardonable Sin

A clarifying word pertaining to the Lord's stern message to the Pharisees about committing the "unpardonable sin" is warranted here. The Lord Jesus stated the following to them:

> *Therefore I say to you, **every sin and blasphemy will be forgiven men, but the blasphemy against the Spirit will not be forgiven men**. Anyone who speaks a word against the Son of Man, it will be forgiven him; but whoever speaks against the Holy Spirit, it will not be forgiven him, **either in this age or in the age to come*** (Matt. 12:31-32, NKJV).

Notice that different forms of sin and blasphemy exist and that forgiveness for these is possible. Secondly, a specific sin entitled *"blasphemy against the Holy Spirit"* is unforgivable, and this specific sin relates to a particular age. "In this age" relates to Christ's public ministry in which He was presently engaged. "The age to come" would relate to His Second Advent to establish His kingdom on earth – the Jewish nation would be restored to Him at that time. In between these ages of Messiah's initial offer and rejection, and second offer and reception, is the Church Age; it is the gap between Daniel's 69th and 70th week of years spoken of in Daniel 9:25-27. During the Church Age, Christ is not personally on the earth declaring the "Kingdom Gospel" message to the lost house of Israel and working miracles to authenticate His message. During the tribulation period, the kingdom message will be again preached (Matt. 24:14), and Christ will return to the earth in great glory, and the nation of Israel shall be converted (Zech. 10:12, Matt. 24:30).

The specific sin that the Pharisees had committed was to ascribe a miracle which Christ had done through the power of the Holy Spirit to Beelzebub, the prince of the demons (Matt. 12:24). These hard-hearted, stiffed-necked, religious leaders had not only rejected the gospel message of Christ and His miracles, but they rendered insults in return for His acts of love and kindness. Because of their intense disbelief which was expressed in disdain for the person of Christ and the working of the Holy Spirit, they had ruthlessly insulted God. On this subject, William MacDonald writes:

> There is reasonable doubt whether the unpardonable sin can be committed today, because He [Christ] is not bodily present performing miracles. The unpardonable sin is not the same as rejecting the gospel; a man may spurn the Saviour for years, then repent, believe and be saved. (Of course, if he dies in unbelief, he remains unforgiven). Nor is the unforgivable sin the same as backsliding; a believer may wander far from the Lord, yet be restored to fellowship in God's family.[3]

Is There an Unpardonable Sin Today?

Some two thousand years ago Jesus Christ tasted death for every man (Heb. 2:9) and was the propitiation for all human sin ever to be committed (1 Jn. 2:2). While the Son was hanging between heaven and earth upon a Roman cross, God the Father judicially punished Him for all human sin. *"There is no more offering for sin"* (Heb. 10:18). It cannot be said, however, that sin is no longer present in the world or that the consequences for sins committed no longer exist – it is, and they do; but from God's point of view, Christ has done all that is necessary for individuals to receive forgiveness for their sins. A person must simply trust Christ as Saviour and receive God's forgiveness. God would be unjust in judging mankind a second time for all their crimes, but one must trust Christ alone to receive the imputed righteousness of God to his or her personal account. Only then does an individual have an acceptable standing with God. You may receive a check for a million dollars, but until you personally endorse the check and deposit it into your bank account, it has no effective value. In the same way, an individual must repent and confess Christ as Saviour to personally receive the efficacy of Calvary.

Repent ye therefore, and be converted, that your sins may be blotted out... (Acts 3:19).

Verily, verily, I say unto you, He that heareth My word, and believeth on Him that sent Me, hath everlasting life, and shall not come into condemnation; but is passed from death unto life (John 5:24).

The Lord Jesus told His disciples that, after He had departed from them, the Holy Spirit would come and comfort them. As the disciples faithfully declared the gospel message to the world, the Holy Spirit would be working with them in the spiritual realm. His ministry would be to exercise the consciences of the unsaved in three ways: to awaken them to their depravity, to their consequential need of a righteous standing before God, and to the judgement of all wickedness. Without the working of the Holy Spirit, it is absolutely impossible for an individual to believe the gospel message, and to come to and follow Christ (1 Cor. 2:9-13).

The sin of the Pharisees was blatant disbelief leading to slander; their rejection of Christ was so intense that the Holy Spirit would no longer work with their consciences to lead them to salvation. They were already dead in their sins and condemned. (Everyone not believing in Christ as Saviour is "condemned already" – John 3:18.) We are born into the world spiritually dead, an inherited state from our fallen forefather Adam (Rom. 5:12). What made the Pharisees' sin so grievous was that God Himself was standing before them, pleading with them to repent and doing wonderful miracles to authenticate the message, yet they refused to believe and even maligned God for His efforts.

Though the sin of disbelief still occurs today, it is my opinion that this specific unpardonable sin cannot be committed today for the Lord is in Glory and not before us preaching and doing miracles in the name of His Father. The fact that an individual is concerned about committing the "unpardonable sin" is proof in itself that he or she can still be forgiven, for the conviction of sin is a work of the Holy Spirit upon the human conscience. One "unforgivable sin" still exists, however – the sin of disbelief (John 16:9)! This sin prevents men from being saved and keeps them out of heaven.

Are You a Blasphemer?

Unfortunately, the answer is "yes," in the sense that we all are guilty of tarnishing the name of the Lord in one way or another. Either in word or deed, we have all communicated disdain for God's name and caused others to do the same. The more mindful we are of honouring God's name, the less likely we will be to possess carefree attitudes which predictably lead to offending God. Paul exhorted the believers at Colosse not to walk as they once did, *"but now ye also put off all these: anger, wrath, malice, blasphemy, filthy communication out of your mouth"* (Col. 3:8). It is natural for an unsaved sinner to blaspheme God for his or her fallen nature is at enmity with God – nothing in it can please God (Rom. 7:18).

However, a true believer has received a new nature and a new life (Gal. 2:20) that cannot sin (1 Jn. 3:9), and that nature seeks to exalt God, which requires putting to death continually the improper lusting of the flesh. In short, we are natural rebels against God, and regrettably, none of us walks as perfectly as he or she should. The reality of the matter is that we blaspheme the name of the Lord in a variety of ways. The tongue is the tail of the heart that wags out of the mouth – the depravity within our hearts, the rebellious nature within, eventually spews out of our mouths (Matt. 12:34-35).

It has already been shown that one can communicate blasphemy against the Lord through speech or other ungodly conduct. The following sins are some specific examples of the different

31

forms of blasphemy – behaviour which makes vain the name of the Lord.

Teaching False Doctrine

Teaching the Word of God to others is both a great privilege and a great responsibility that ultimately has accountability with God. Regarding this reality, James warned, *"My brethren, let not many of you become teachers, knowing that we shall receive a stricter judgment"* (Jas. 3:1, NKVJ). When a teacher opens the oracles of God to speak, he speaks for God. When an individual perverts the Word of God through traditions of men, vain philosophies, flawed music, or ignorance, he has misrepresented God and slandered God's name. Consider Paul's message to Timothy:

> *If any man teach otherwise, and consent not to wholesome words, even the words of our Lord Jesus Christ, and to the doctrine which is according to godliness; he is proud, knowing nothing, but doting about questions and strifes of words, whereof cometh envy, strife, railings, evil surmisings* (1 Tim. 6:3-4).

"Railings" in the passage is translated from the same Greek word normally rendered "blasphemy." An individual who teaches false doctrine commits blasphemy against God because he or she perverts truth, thus, causing God's holiness and perfection to be diminished and/or distorted in the minds of those listening.

Swearing Falsely

To swear is to strongly affirm a promise or statement by using the Lord's name. The activity of swearing to validate a promise was quite common in the Old Testament. The normal Hebrew word for swearing, *shaba*, which means "to swear'" or "to take an oath," is found 180 times in the Old Testament.

In the New Testament, however, the Lord Jesus traversed the high moral ground on the subject of swearing. He instructed His disciples, *"But let your communication be, Yea, yea; Nay, nay: for whatsoever is more than these cometh of evil"* (Matt. 5:37). The disciple of Christ does not need to swear to validate his or her words; the merit of everything said should be wholesome, accurate, needful and gracious without adding God's name to it. Hence, the Lord issued a stern warning, *"But I say unto you, **that every idle word** that men shall speak, they shall give account thereof in the day of judgment. For by thy words thou shalt be justified, and by thy words thou shalt be condemned"* (Matt. 12:36-37). Lord, please forgive us for all our idle chit-chat and for allowing our tongues to flap in the wind!

Swearing involves tying God's name to our statements in an attempt to better validate what we say – to heighten the credibility of our words. The believer should not engage in such practices, for to do so would certainly bring low the name of God. Listen to James' warning for this sin, *"But above all things, my brethren, swear not, neither by heaven, neither by the earth, neither by any other oath: but let your yea be yea; and your nay, nay; lest ye fall into condemnation"* (Jas. 5:12). Demeaning the name of the Lord by swearing falsely is a terrible thing. As we are forgetful creatures and are rarely perfect in our speech, it behooves us to refrain from swearing oaths which we will most assuredly fall short of keeping. Certainly, the rash vows of Jephthah (Judg. 11:29-40) and Herod (Acts 12:20-23) serve as historical examples of the heavy price to be paid when one foolishly swears to God to do something.

An individual may be put into a position, such as in a court of law, where they would be placed under oath. These situations are rare, but sometimes are unavoidable. Perjury is a form of blasphemy, so if you are put "under oath," be diligent not to defame the Lord's name. *"And ye shall not swear by My name falsely, neither shalt thou profane the name of Thy God: I am the Lord"* (Lev. 19:12) Swearing falsely has its consequences, for God does not forget:

> *"I will send out the curse,"* says the Lord of hosts; *"It shall enter the house of the thief and the house of the one who swears falsely by My name"* (Zech. 5:4, NKJV).

The believer should always do his or her best to convey meaningful and accurate speech and to refrain from idle talk. *"Let no corrupt communication proceed out of your mouth, but that which is good to the use of edifying, that it may minister grace unto the hearers"* (Eph. 4:29). Solomon wisely concluded regarding the operation of our speech, *"Be not rash with thy mouth, and let not thine heart be hasty to utter any thing before God: for God is in heaven, and thou upon earth: therefore let thy words be few"* (Eccl. 5:2). May all our profane speech be replaced with praise!

Stealing

"Lest I be full and deny You, and say, 'Who is the Lord?' Or lest I be poor and steal, and profane the name of my God" (Prov. 30:9, NKJV). The writer requested that he neither be rich (fearing he might forget the Lord) nor poor such that he might be forced to steal and, in so doing, disdain God's name. For this cause Paul exhorts believers to pursue the same Christ-honouring behaviour: *"Let him that stole steal no more: but rather let him labour, working with his hands the thing which is good, that he may have to give to him that needeth"* (Eph. 4:28). The Law was kept when one refrained from stealing, but the fulfilling of the law was accomplished through giving, not by not stealing (Rom. 13:8).

Proverbs illustrates that individuals can communicate blasphemy for the Lord's name without using actual words. We often say to our children, "actions speak louder than words," but we probably don't reckon the same truth in our breaking of God's laws. The believer sins because he or she chooses to, and our rebel behaviour insults God, affronts His holy character and blasphemes His name. We cannot claim to be a Christian (a Christ-one) while we are diminishing His name through un-Christlike conduct. Often, we think more about the personal consequences of our sin than we do about the hurt inflicted on the heart of God. Stealing offends God and degrades His name in the eyes of the unsaved.

Demoting the Character of God

One would have to wonder if anything pleases Satan more than when men curse and blaspheme the Lord. Peter engaged in intense cursing and repeated denial of the Lord while Christ was on trial; he found out just how weak his carnal weapons were against his flesh and the wiles of the devil. His cowardice and thoughts of self-preservation undermined the name of Christ (Matt. 26:74).

In the case of Job, twice Satan told God that *"he (Job) will curse Thee to Thy face"* (Job. 1:11; 2:5) if he were allowed to assault Job. Unfortunately, this very idea was given to Job by his wife, *"curse God and die"* (Job 2:9). Satan thoroughly enjoys dishonouring God and His name. Often overwhelming circumstances will cause a child of God to lose hope and lapse in his or her faith – strong faith is required to trust the hand which originated the billows and waves of adversity that crash upon our heads. Please note that God began the conversation with Satan concerning His servant Job. In other words, God nominated Job! The next nominee could be you or me.

Although Job did not curse God, he did sin against the Lord during his distress. The matter angered Bildad, and he reproved Job during their first dialogue (Job 8:1-7). What was the sin? Bildad accused Job of blaspheming God – speaking ill of God by questioning and accusing God of "wrongdoing." Though Bildad was a miserable counselor and consoler to Job, on this point the basis for his rebuke was correct, though not warranted; for God would personally address the matter with His servant Job later (Job 38).

Bildad's error was in informing Job that all his difficulties were a result of personal sin against God: *"God will not cast away a perfect man, neither will he help the evildoers"* (Job 8:20, also 8:6). However, this was not the circumstance at all; Job's trial was not the chastening judgement of God resulting from Job's personal sin. God was obtaining glory out of Job's situation, while at the same time, further refining His servant who Scripture declares *"was blameless and upright, and one that feared God, and shunned evil"* (Job 1:1, NKJV). On two separate occasions, God met with Job in a whirlwind to address his wrong attitudes – Job witnessed the holy and awesome nature of God first-hand. God's very character defines what is right; thus, He can do only what is pure, right and holy. God's very character is perfect moral light and whatever is in darkness is not of God – the lack of God's rightness is the definition of evil (Isa. 45:5-7). The holiness of God enabled Job to better understand that God is righteous in all His ways.

During arduous circumstances, it is all too easy for the downcast and disheartened soul to think and say evil of God's doings. The fact is that God loves us too much to permit us to remain the way we are – He greatly desires for us to reflect the moral glory of His Son to a world that desperately needs to see Christ. Aggressive chiseling, chipping, sanding and polishing are required to transform a chunk of granite into an attractive sculpture – and often God labors with hearts harder than granite. Our God is a God of promises, and we must simply trust Him in such arduous times and not question His character – He does have a plan, and it is marvelous:

For I know the thoughts that I think toward you, says the Lord, thoughts of peace and not of evil, to give you a future and a hope (Jer. 29:11, NKJV).

And we know that all things work together for good to them that love God, to them who are the called according to His purpose (Rom. 8:28).

There hath no temptation taken you but such as is common to man: but God is faithful, who will not suffer you to be tempted above that ye are able; but will with the temptation also make a way to escape, that ye may be able to bear it (1 Cor. 10:13).

If there was no God, our present sufferings would be overwhelming, for we would be a people without hope. But knowing that God is in all our woes and that He is personally working each out for our good and His glory affords joy in tribulations! In trials, let us maintain the up-look and not be guilty of looking down on God.

The Impudent Heart

In His pungent "Woe" message to the Pharisees, the Lord Jesus addressed the hypocritical act of swearing in a way which degraded the name of the Lord. Although under a different guise, the same behaviour is often witnessed today. The Lord said:

Woe unto you, ye blind guides, which say, Whosoever shall swear by the temple, it is nothing; but whosoever shall swear by the gold of the temple, he is a debtor! Ye fools and blind: for whether is greater, the gold, or the temple that sanctifieth the gold? And, Whosoever shall swear by the altar, it is nothing;

but whosoever sweareth by the gift that is upon it, he is guilty.
Ye fools and blind: for whether is greater, the gift, or the altar
that sanctifieth the gift? Whoso therefore shall swear by the al-
tar, sweareth by it, and by all things thereon. And whoso shall
swear by the temple, sweareth by it, and by Him that dwelleth
therein. And he that shall swear by heaven, sweareth by the
throne of God, and by Him that sitteth thereon (Matt. 23:16-22).

In esteeming the gold band that adorned the pinnacle of the
temple more than the temple itself, the Pharisees were demonstrating disdain for God. Where is the value? In the gold or the
temple? In the offering or the altar? The Lord bluntly told them
that the altar gave value to the sacrifice, and that the temple bestowed the honour to the gold. The altar and the temple were
patterned after holy heavenly realities (Heb. 9:23); each was directly connected to God. In placing the value on the offering and
the gold, the Pharisees had disassociated themselves from God,
but the Lord was telling them that only that which is connected
with God has value; their traditions and swearing were just human nonsense and an insult to God.

The highest honour for gold would have been to be used in
the house of God. The highest honour of a lamb in Judea was to
be used as a sacrifice on the bronze altar. If gold and sheep had
ambition, this would have been their highest calling. Christ was
teaching that man apart from his connection with God is nothing; ambition apart from God is nothing; abilities apart from
God are nothing! The only reason a believer can be honoured
before God is because of his or her association with Jesus Christ.
Spurgeon once said to a believer, "The greatest thing about you
is your connection with Calvary [Christ]."

The Lord Jesus wants our motives, our abilities and our entire life to be connected with Him. It is possible for us to ignorantly commit the same form of blasphemy that the Pharisees did
(i.e. undervaluing our association with Christ). For example, the

reader might have a brilliant mind. Some might say, "The Lord would be fortunate to have a mind like yours in His service." Wrong! That which is in association with Christ is what has the value. The right thinking is: "my greatest privilege in life is to use my talents for the Lord." Your intellect does not sanctify Jesus Christ, but Jesus Christ sanctifies your mind for His purpose and glory. Only those abilities that are submitted to the Lord can be used to honour Him and to bless the body of Christ.

Some time ago I heard William MacDonald tell the following story, I share it with you to illustrate the application of the Lord's message to the Pharisees:

> A number of years ago, while touring Paris, an American found an amber necklace in a second-hand street shop. It was marked with a low price, so he bought it. However, the customs officials really socked it to him with a duty tax when he reentered the US, which aroused his suspicion. He went to a jeweler who estimated its worth to be $25,000. He went to a second gemologist who said the necklace was worth $30,000. The man, being astounded, asked why it was worth so much. The jeweler handed him the magnifying glass and told him where to look on the necklace, where he read the inscription: "To Josephine from Napoleon." The necklace was not worth $30,000 in itself, but its association with Josephine and Napoleon made it valuable.

The same is true of you, dear believer. You only have value because of your association with Christ. We should not mock His Lordship and defame His name by thinking we have some ability or talent that He would do well to value and use. Such thinking is nothing less than hypocrisy and a pharisaical expression of pride – a form of blasphemy! Our highest service to the Lord is to be a living sacrifice, an emptied vessel of honour (2 Tim. 2:21) fitted for His sovereign use. If we live a holy consecrated life – He will honour Himself; we need not presuppose our profitability to God.

In what ways might Christians be committing the same distorted thinking? Christian terminology or music which devalues the person and work of Christ or our association with Christ should be corrected. Continuously saying or singing something which is wrong, even if the matter seems trivial to us, in time becomes perceived truth in our thinking. The distinction between reality and fantasy becomes blurred when awareness to Scriptural truth is supplanted with indiscriminate familiarities.

As this is a sensitive subject with some, I will merely introduce two of several often overlooked distinctions of the believer's association with Christ in the form of questions. Is Jesus our Friend, or are we His Friends? Secondly, is Jesus our Brother, or are we His brethren? Scripture always conveys the thought of us being the Lord's friends and His brethren, not the opposite association.

The only person in the entire Bible to be directly called "a friend of God" is Abraham (2 Chron. 20:7; Isa. 41:8; Jas. 2:23). In Exodus 33:11 we read, *"So the Lord spoke to Moses face to face, as a man speaks to his friend"* (NKJV). John the Baptist spoke of *"the friend of the Bridegroom"* (John 3:29) or "the Bridegroom's friend." While speaking to His disciples, the Lord Jesus referred to Lazarus as *"our friend"* (John 11:11), and later, He also called those who believed on Him and obeyed His word "friends" (John 15:13-15). Friendship involves selfless ministry, and Christ demonstrated at Calvary His sacrificial love for His friends. As far as distorting the proper focus, it was the Pharisees, not believers, which said of the Lord, *"Behold a man gluttonous, and a winebibber, a friend of publicans and sinners"* (Matt. 11:19).

As with the friend terminology, no reference may be found in Scripture which implies that Christ is our brother; we are His brethren (Matt. 12:50; 23:8). Why? *"For both He that sanctifieth and they who are sanctified are all of one: for which cause **He is not ashamed to call them brethren**"* (Heb. 2:11). We are set apart in Him to enjoy an intimate relationship with Him; He is not set apart by us! In speaking to the Pharisees, the Lord clarified the matter of who His brethren were – those who would submit to God's will and honour Him:

> *Who is **My** mother, or **My** brethren? And He looked round about on them which sat about Him, and said, Behold **My** mother and **My** brethren!* ***For whosoever shall do the will of God, the same is My brother,*** *and **My** sister, and mother (Mark 3:33-35).*

It is Christ's connection with us that ensures fellowship, not our familiarity with Him. The receipt of His love consequently prompts our allegiance and devotion to Him (1 Jn. 4:19) – we prove we are His brethren and friends through obedience. Referring to Christ as our friend is an innocent expression, but in effect unintentionally lowers Him to our station. Which sounds better: "I am a friend of the President," or "the President is my friend?" The answer is the former. By being his friend, I relate to him in his position of authority, whereas if he were just my friend, I would lower him to my common social position as a "nobody."

There is no desire to place an undue burden on the Lord's people by strictly legalizing these scriptural distinctions in our terminology. The old hymns *What a Friend We Have in Jesus* and *I've Found a Friend* contain lovely lyrics – I enjoy singing them too, and don't want to imply that the reader is blaspheming the Lord Jesus by singing them. In the same way, perhaps it is permissible for the believer to *apply* Proverbs 18:24 *"there is a friend that sticketh closer than a brother"* to the Lord Jesus – for He has proven Himself friendly. My point in reviewing the terminology is this – the Holy Spirit was completely specific for a reason. The ministry of the Holy Spirit is to guide us into all truth and to glorify the Lord Jesus (John 16:13-14). The exactness of Scripture reflects the Holy Spirit's work to prevent casual speech which might ignorantly undermine our responsibility to Him or His association with us. His exalted position and our responsibility to Him in thought and deed are vitally important.

Consider the second stanza of a well-known praise chorus entitled *As the Deer*: "You're my friend and You are my brother even though You are my King." The wording has always bothered me, but not until recently did I understand why. The exalted title of the Lord is secondary, while the lowering of Christ to our station is primary. I am certainly not questioning the writer's devotion to Christ; surely no dishonour was intended, yet the phraseology is clearly unbiblical. It is a nice song and the remaining words are Christ-honouring, but this blemish in the second stanza unfortunately diminishes our thinking of Christ as Lord – the biblical focus of the *friend* and *brethren* terminology is not His friendliness to us, but our responsibility to be His friends and brethren (i.e. to do His will).

So carrying these examples further, what might be the consequences of "my Brother" or "my Friend" terminology when speaking of the Lord. Granted these particular cases are not as critical as some, but unbiblical expressions relating to God have proven in time to soften our appreciation for truth and our reverence for Him. A few years ago I was doing visitation work and spoke to an individual who responded to the gospel message this way, "Jesus and I are tight ... He is my friend," but the woman later admitted to having an immoral lifestyle. Obviously, she was not Jesus' friend – as His friends do the will of the Father. Many claim to be associated with God, but not submitted to God – terminology does matter. As another example, a believer reported to me that a preacher, during a recent Sunday morning message, exhorted the congregation "All of you need to know your big Brother," speaking of the Lord Jesus Christ.

Shall Christians call upon the Lord of all in such a casual way and by a title not found in Scripture? Doesn't this practice violate the second of the Ten Commandments? Man is creating an imaginary image of God which fits his liking. It may not be a golden calf, but neither is it the Lord revealed in Scripture. Beloved of the Lord, in these days of rampant deception and wickedness, we do well just to affirm God's revelation of Himself. Let us continuously review and evaluate our terminology lest in time, unbiblical expressions cause us to err unknowingly and to devalue His association with us, His person or His Lordship.

While warning the Christians of Galatia not to adopt a doctrine of legalism as a means of maintaining their salvation, Paul emphasized the proper point of view concerning knowing God: *"When ye knew not God, ye did service unto them which by nature are no gods. But now, after **that ye have known God, or rather are known of God**, how turn ye again to the weak and beggarly elements, whereunto ye desire again to be in bondage?"* (Gal. 4:8-9). Being personally known of God, not knowing God brings salvation, but we will certainly know Him, if He knows us as His friends. Experientially knowing God is evident by a changed and yielded life, in this way our association as His friends and brethren is proven. Any other way than submission and obedience leads to an impudent heart and pharisaical pride!

Causing Others to Blaspheme God

Besides committing the grievous act of blasphemy itself, Christians should avoid conduct that would provoke others to blaspheme the name of the Lord. There are occasions in which living blamelessly will undoubtly require a believer to sacrifice his or her liberty in Christ as to not hinder the gospel message before the unsaved (1 Cor. 9:12, 10:33). But the vast majority of situations in which a Christian prompts an unsaved person to blaspheme the Lord could be avoided if the believer just pursued holy living.

You say, "How can I cause another to blaspheme the Lord?" The following are scriptural examples and are by no means an exhaustive list:

Claiming to be God's people, but not keeping His commandments.

Thou that makest thy boast of the law, through breaking the law dishonourest thou God? For the name of God is blasphemed among the Gentiles through you, as it is written (Rom. 2:23-24).

Personal conduct, which even God's enemies know to be immoral.

And David said unto Nathan, I have sinned against the LORD. And Nathan said unto David, The LORD also hath put away thy sin; thou shalt not die. Howbeit, because by this deed thou hast given great occasion to the enemies of the LORD to blaspheme; the child also that is born unto thee shall surely die (2 Sam. 12:13-14).

Husbands and fathers who do not provide for their families.

But if any provide not for his own, and specially for those of his own house, he hath denied the faith, and is worse than an infidel (1 Tim. 5:8).

William MacDonald writes:

When a Christian fails to do this, he denies by his actions the very truths which Christianity teaches. Such a person is worse than an unbeliever for the simple reason that many unbelievers show loving care for their own relatives. Also, a Christian can thus bring reproach on the name of the Lord in a way that an unbeliever cannot do.[1]

Wives and mothers who do not keep the home.

That they may teach the young women to be sober, to love their husbands, to love their children, to be discreet, chaste, keepers at home, good, obedient to their own husbands, that the word of God be not blasphemed (Titus 2:4-5).

I will therefore that the younger women marry, bear children, guide the house, give none occasion to the adversary to speak reproachfully (1 Tim. 5:14).

Disrespect to civil order.

Let as many servants as are under the yoke count their own masters worthy of all honour, that the name of God and His doctrine be not blasphemed (1 Tim. 6:1).

Let every soul be subject unto the higher powers. For there is no power but of God: the powers that be are ordained of God. Whosoever therefore resisteth the power, resisteth the ordinance of God: and they that resist shall receive to themselves damnation (Rom. 13:1-2).

The sum of all these things is that associating ourselves with Christ but then defying His Lordship in action causes the Lord's name to be degraded in the world's eyes. Sinning while standing in the light of truth ensures that the believer's sin will be more noticeable to others! Instead of being a testimony and showing forth the glory of Christ, we will cause His name to be blasphemed by the unsaved. Do you cause others to blaspheme the name of the Lord? Blasphemy is a serious sin, for it diminishes God in human reckoning. Blasphemy causes the One who created all, controls all and imparted His best for humanity to be considered less than He is.

Oswald Chambers described the commonly committed sin of blasphemy by Christians:

Beware of worshiping Jesus as the Son of God and professing your faith in Him as the Saviour of the world, while you blaspheme Him by the complete evidence in your daily life that He is powerless to do anything in and through you.[2]

The Lord said to His disciples, *"And why call ye Me, Lord, Lord, and do not the things which I say?"* (Luke 6:46). The Lord did not want His name defamed in the world by hypocritical lip service; He wanted totally committed disciples, for anything less is not biblical discipleship. He is Lord of all, and true disciples acknowledge it!

Polycarp, a second century elder in the church at Smyrna, understood that it was possible to blaspheme God not only through speech, but in actions also. When the Proconsul threatened to burn him alive unless he recanted his allegiance to Jesus Christ, Polycarp told his executioners: "Eighty-six years I have served Him, and He has done me no wrong. How can I blaspheme my King who has saved me?" Indeed he did not blaspheme God, but was martyred for Christ sake.[3]

The prophet Isaiah captures the true essence of loyalty to God and His name, *"the desire of our soul is to Thy name"* (Isa. 26:8). Dear reader, can you say that this is your conviction? Is the desire of your soul to uphold the name of God in all that you do and say? If so, revisit the above checklist to ensure that your attitudes, motives, speech, and behaviour are not causing the name of the Lord God to be blasphemed. If your answer is "no," thanks for being honest, but please prudently ponder the following passages of Scripture:

> *But whosoever shall deny Me before men, him will I also deny before My Father which is in heaven* (Matt. 10:33).

> *If we suffer, we shall also reign with Him: if we deny Him, He also will deny us* (2 Tim. 2:12).

In the same way that the Lord commissioned Paul, He speaks to every true believer: you are *"a chosen vessel unto Me, **to bear My name before**..."* (Acts 9:15). Paul faithfully declared the name of Jesus Christ before the Gentiles, kings, and the children of Israel. The Church is commanded to go forth *"and teach all nations, baptizing them **in the name of the Father, and of the Son, and of the Holy Ghost [Spirit]**, teaching them to observe*

48

all things whatsoever I have commanded you..." (Matt. 28:19-20). When you evaluate the options for living life, only two choices become evident: live to bear up the name of the Lord, or live in such a way that causes others to blaspheme His name. Does your life cause others to blaspheme that name of God?

The above sins are just a sampling of a much larger list of ways people blaspheme the name of God. Often, when we get caught in sin, our first inclination is to behave like Jacob after the terrible events at Shechem (Gen. 34) – we are concerned about how our wrongdoings will affect us and what others will think about us. Such a thought pattern in itself indicates contempt for God. When a well-known preacher is found to be engaging in gross moral sin, our first response should be to grieve over the shame levied upon Christ's name. When an assembly of God's people splits over personality issues, we should all grieve for the poor testimony of Christ in that community. It is time that the Church bring the name of the Lord Jesus Christ into the forefront of our thinking and quit being selfish and blasphemous in our religiosity.

Why did David charge a giant named Goliath in battle? The honour of God's name was at stake! The people were unconcerned that the name of their God was brought into disrepute, but David felt the matter keenly. *"Then said David to the Philistine, Thou comest to me with a sword, and with a spear, and with a shield: but I come to thee in the name of the Lord of hosts, the God of the armies of Israel, whom thou hast defied"* (1 Sam. 17:45). David courageously defended the Lord's name because he understood that *"the name of the Lord is a strong tower; the righteous run to it and are safe"* (Prov. 18:10, NKJV). Likewise, our conduct must consider Christ and His name first in all things, for we are His saints. Paul understood the value of this identification: *"But fornication, and all uncleanness, or covetousness, **let it not be once named among you as becometh saints**"* (Eph. 5:3).

Believers compose the household of God, His living temple on earth to shine forth His virtue; God forbid that we disdain His name before the nations. Charles Spurgeon forcibly conveys this point:

> Professor! Is sin subdued in you? If your life is unholy your heart is unchanged, and if your heart is unchanged you are an unsaved person. If the Saviour has not sanctified you, renewed you, given you a hatred of sin and a love of holiness, He has done nothing in you of a saving character. The grace which does not make a man better than others is a worthless counterfeit. Christ saves His people, not in their sins, but from them. "Without holiness no man shall see the Lord." ***"Let every one that nameth the name of Christ depart from iniquity."*** If not saved from sin, how shall we hope to be counted among His people. Lord, save me now from all evil, and enable me to honour my Saviour.[4]

King Solomon erected a magnificent house for the Lord, the temple. When it was dedicated, Solomon prayed: *"that all people of the earth may know Thy name, to fear Thee, as do Thy people ..."* (1 Kgs. 8:43). If the unsaved masses are to be reached for Christ in this present day, the Church must rethink its careless attitudes regarding how it represents and proclaims the name of Christ. Deliberate disregard for the Word of God, complacency over sin, and loss of reverence for the Lord's name have degraded the name of Christ throughout the world. The Church desperately needs revival! May we all repent and again esteem Christ above all things, *"that in all things He might have the preeminence"* (Col. 1:18), and may we fervently pray as Solomon did so long ago: *"that all people of the earth may know Thy name, to fear Thee, as do Thy people."*

Rightly Using the Lord's Name

God understands our natural limitations in comprehending spiritual and eternal matters. As a declaration of grace to us, He used various literary forms in the Old Testament, including word-pictures, prophecies, shadows, types, allegories, symbols, and plain language, to prelude the revelation of His supreme gift of love to the world – His own Son. Then, in the New Testament, God, demonstrating His infinite wisdom, created a new and vivid literary form to express the grandeur of His Son's life and sacrifice. By this new literary form, *gospel*, God revealed His Son as the visible message of salvation to mankind. The four gospel accounts, each with own their distinct and unique vantage points, present the Lord Jesus Christ in the manner by which His Father chose to reveal Him.

It is no wonder, then, that the name of Jesus is found 625 times in the Gospels, compared with 358 times in the remainder of the New Testament. The Lord pervades and is indeed the gospel message itself – He was both the message and messenger in one. In all, the name of "Jesus" is found nearly one thousand times in the New Testament. "Jesus" is actually derived from two Hebrew words compounded to mean "Jehovah's Salvation." Literally, "Jehovah saves" through Jesus. How important is the name of Jesus Christ? Peter speaking of Christ said, *"Neither is there salvation in any other: for there is none other name under heaven given among men, whereby we must be saved"* (Acts 4:12).

The Epistles are addressed to those who know Christ as Saviour; therefore, the exalted tone, the reverential speech and connected titles of authority are expected. He is more than a man named Jesus to the believer; He is Lord and Saviour. The apostles, guided by the Holy Spirit, were very careful in declaring the Lord's name. Their example is a good one for all believers to follow – let us speak and write of the Lord Jesus in an honourable fashion.

Though many Christians are not conscious of using the Lord's name inappropriately, many do so and do it on a daily basis. Because the believer is to bear up the name of the Lord to the world, we don't want to ignorantly tarnish or devalue the only name by which mankind can be saved. In this chapter, we will examine Scripture to determine how to properly address the Lord Jesus whether before the throne of grace or before others.

"His Name was Called Jesus" (Lk. 2:21)

It is observed that the Gospels introduce the man Jesus as God's Saviour of humanity, while the Epistles, written after Christ's glorification, declare more fully His inherent greatness and exalted position over all creation. This transition of tone can be noted in the use of the Lord's given name, Jesus, in Scripture. For example: The Gospels contain only one reference to any title preceding the name of "Jesus," that being the *"Lord Jesus"* (Lk. 24:3). He is personally addressed as "Jesus Christ" only five times in the Gospels. In all, only six occurrences of the 625 references to the name "Jesus" in the Gospel accounts directly connect a title of exaltation to His name.

In the same way, the Gospels record the message of Christ before the crucifixion to the lost house of Israel, and the book of Acts accounts the preaching of Jesus to a lost Gentile world. However, the exaltation of Jesus Christ is quite evident in the Epistles, which explains the glorious mysteries of God concerning salvation, and in the book of the Revelation, which declares Christ's authority over all things. Of the 290 times the proper name "Jesus" is found, 263 references are associated with a dignified title. Here is the breakdown:

Name/Title	Occurrences in Epistles and Revelation
Jesus Christ (only)	82
Lord Jesus Christ	78
Christ Jesus (only)	55
Lord Jesus (only)	20
Jesus our Lord	7
Jesus Christ our Lord	9
Saviour Jesus Christ	6
Christ Jesus the Lord	2
Jesus is the Christ	2
Jesus the Son of God	1
Jesus is the Lord	1
	Total = 263

Of the twenty-seven remaining references to "Jesus," ten have direct connection with God the Father and two with the Holy Spirit, seven exalt Christ within the same sentence and two occurrences do so within the same thought, and six are miscellaneous references. The following is the detailed analysis:

Association with the Father: Rom. 3:26; 1 Thess. 1:10; 1 Thess. 4:14 (2); Heb. 2:9; Heb. 7:21-22; Heb. 12:2; Rev. 14:12; Rev. 19:10 (2)

Association with the Holy Spirit: Rom. 8:11; 1 Cor. 12:3

Christ dignified by title in same sentence: 2 Cor. 4:5; 2 Cor. 4:10; 2 Cor. 4:14; Eph. 4:21; Heb. 6:20; Rev. 20:4; Rev. 22:16

Christ exalted by title within same thought: 2 Cor. 4:11 (2 references connected with 2 Cor. 4:10).

Miscellaneous:
2 Cor. 11:4 (preach another Jesus);
Heb. 4:8 (refers to Joshua);
Heb. 10:19 (Jesus' blood);
Heb. 12:24 (Jesus the mediator of new covenant – with sprinkling of blood);
Heb. 13:12 (the body of Jesus judged outside the gate);
Rev. 17:6 (martyrs of Jesus).

Concerning these miscellaneous references to the name of "Jesus" Sir Robert Anderson concludes:

And the more we investigate it, the plainer will the proof appear, that while throughout the Gospels the Lord is habitually called "Jesus," "the simple name" is never used in the Epistles, save with some peculiar significance either of doctrine or of emphasis.[1]

Epistles are wisdom books, through which God reveals mysteries to mankind that have been concealed within the vastness of His mind since the foundation of the world. In these writings, the apostles are very careful when speaking the Lord's name to honour Him with a connected title, or directly associating Him with the Godhead, or exalting Him directly in speech. Only in the rare instances, which refer back to the Lord's earthly pathway (i.e. speaking of Jesus' shed blood and body sacrificed) does His name stand alone. It is plausible that in some instances, such as 1 Thessalonians 1:10, where a direct title of exaltation is not connected to "Jesus" that the purpose was to remind the believers of the literal meaning of His name – "Jehovah's salvation." Though Paul does esteem Christ through referencing His association with the Father in this verse, perhaps he intended to provoke the suffering saints at Thessalonica to trust in Christ alone – "Jehovah's salvation" would deliver them from the wrath to come.

A brief evaluation of the book of Romans will vividly demonstrate how carefully the apostles treated the name of Jesus Christ. Paul refers directly to the name of "Jesus" thirty-eight times in Romans, and thirty-six of those times he ties *Christ* or *Lord*, or both, with His name. The two remaining occurrences of "Jesus" appear without an associated title because the text associates Jesus intimately with God the Father (Rom. 3:26) and the Holy Spirit (Rom. 8:11). The Lord is not superior to the other members of the Godhead; however, He does possess full association and equality with Them. Paul spoke of Jesus as Christ and as Lord in regards to His relationship to humanity and His ministry for mankind, but no title was compounded with Jesus when speaking of Christ's association with the Godhead.

Why the varying titles? Often, the first word of the Lord's title punctuates the truth that a particular passage of Scripture is conveying. If the truth mainly has to do with the Lordship of Christ, then "Lord" is the first word. When the Lord's humanity is in view, quite often "Jesus" is the first word.

The blind man's experience recorded in John 9 serves as a good example of how one's understanding of who Jesus is affects how one addresses Him. After the Lord had healed the man born blind, those who knew him asked how he had received his sight. *"He answered and said, **A man that is called Jesus** made clay, and anointed mine eyes, and said unto me, Go to the pool of Siloam, and wash: and I went and washed, and I received* *sight"* (John 9:11). Later, the healed blind man was brought before the Pharisees to be interrogated.

> *Then again the Pharisees also asked him how he had received his sight. He said unto them, He put clay upon mine eyes, and I washed, and do see. Therefore said some of the Pharisees, This man is not of God, because he keepeth not the Sabbath day. Others said, How can a man that is a sinner do such miracles? And there was a division among them. They say unto the blind man again, What sayest thou of him, that he hath opened thine eyes? He said, **He is a prophet** (John 9:15-17).*

After the Pharisees had excommunicated the healed blind man from Judaism, the Lord Jesus personally sought him out.

> *Jesus heard that they had cast him out; and when He had found him, He said unto him, Dost thou believe on the Son of God? He answered and said, Who is he, Lord, that I might believe on him? And Jesus said unto him, Thou hast both seen Him, and it is He that talketh with thee. And **he said, Lord, I believe. And he worshipped Him** (John 9:35-38).*

Notice the progressive understanding of who "Jesus" was to the blind man: a man named Jesus, a prophet, the Son of God, his Lord. The healed blind man did not worship the Lord Jesus for what He had done for him, but for whom the Lord was. Do you think he would ever have called the Son of God just a man named "Jesus" after he knew who He truly was? No, in fact, no example appears in Scripture of a disciple of Christ personally addressing the Lord Jesus only by His given name "Jesus." Why? To the disciple, Jesus is "Christ," "Lord," "Teacher," "Master," and "Son of God"; He is much more than just an acquaintance and much more than just a man named Jesus!

In a future day, all the wicked will be resurrected, and positioned before Jesus Christ at the Great White Throne of God (Rev. 20:11). Their agonizing response will be immediate; they shall bow the knee to Him. Though their mouths will be stopped because of the convicting evidence against them (Rom. 3:19), their tongues when loosened will confess *that Jesus Christ is Lord.*

Wherefore God also hath highly exalted Him, and given Him a name which is above every name: That at the name of Jesus every knee should bow, of things in heaven, and things in earth, and things under the earth; And that every tongue should confess that Jesus Christ is Lord, to the glory of God the Father (Phil. 2:9-11).

At that moment of reckoning, Jesus Christ will be far more than a man to them; He will be known as their Lord and Judge! Those who chose not to honour Him in life and receive eternal life, will honour Him in judgement and receive eternal death.

Who addressed the Lord Jesus by His given name after understanding who He claimed to be? The Pharisees and the demons – namely those who rejected Christ's rule over them. Why did Judas never call Christ "Lord?" Because he did not recognize the Lord's rule over him. Paul precisely identifies the spiritual issue: *"Therefore I make known to you that no one speaking by the Spirit of God calls Jesus accursed, and no one can say that Jesus is Lord except by the Holy Spirit"* (1 Cor 12:3, NJKV). Those who have not been born again will not be compelled to declare Christ as Lord! But those who have life in Him are compelled to honour Him in their speech. Ponder Paul's use of titles and exaltation in the opening salutation to those gathered in the Lord Jesus' name at Corinth:

*Unto the church of God which is at Corinth, to them that are sanctified in **Christ Jesus**, called to be saints, with all that in* *every place call upon the name of **Jesus Christ our Lord**, both theirs and ours: Grace be unto you, and peace, from God our Father, and from **the Lord Jesus Christ**. I thank my God always on your behalf, for the grace of God which is given you by **Jesus Christ**; that in every thing ye are enriched by him, in all utterance, and in all knowledge; even as the testimony of **Christ** was confirmed in you: So that ye come behind in no gift; waiting for the coming of our **Lord Jesus Christ**: Who shall also confirm you unto the end, that ye may be blameless in the day of our **Lord Jesus Christ**. God is faithful, by whom ye were called unto the fellowship of his **Son Jesus Christ our Lord** (1 Cor. 1:2-9).*

Some might think, "Paul, you went a bit overboard with your usage of Christ and Lord while talking about the Saviour Jesus; we know who He is." Paul was speaking to a carnal church that needed God's order in their assembly, and he initiated a series of exhortations by affirming the Head of the Church and the Church's submission to Him. When God's people let divine headship slip, devaluing of God-ordained order and conduct soon follow, and in the end, the blessing of God is lost.

Do you see how important it is to use the name of Jesus properly? Dear believer, don't superficially use His name – it is precious and is a name highly honoured in heaven. Don't demean Him by referring to Him merely as a man when you know He deserves much more recognition. He is more than "the man upstairs" as some glibly refer to the Lord Jesus Christ!

Accentuating this critical point, T. Ernest Wilson, a long-term missionary (with his wife Elizabeth) in Angola, once implored attendees at a Bible Conference:

My dear brother, sister, if you are ever speaking to Him in prayer, or you are ever speaking about Him in the ministry of the Word, or in the proclamation of the gospel give Him His rightful title.... He is the Lord Jesus Christ.... Every intelligent believer today, speaking to Him reverently, will use that title the Lord Jesus Christ."[2]

We often hear men concluding their prayers with "in Jesus' name, Amen," or "in Jesus' name we pray, Amen." Should we speak so casually of the Lord while addressing His Father, the very one who has exalted His Son above all powers, thrones and dominions? Which of us would address the Queen of England or the President of the United States by their first name? If you knew the President when he was ten years old – calling him by his given name would be expected. However, to refer to some- one in high authority in such a casual way would be disrespect- ful. How much more inappropriate is it to refer to the Lord of all by addressing Him by His name given at birth and to ignore the full climax of His revelation.

It is not to say that the essence of the name *Jesus* does not convey special significance, for it does. As mentioned earlier, "Jesus" is translated from *Iesous* in the Greek which is derived from two Hebrew words: *Yehovah* and *yasha`* which means "to deliver or to save." Literally, *Jesus* is "Jehovah's salvation." When we utter the name "Jesus," we are referring to the sacred covenant name of God in the English language. "Jesus" is a spe- cial name. It was by that name God declared His gift to the World, His Son, who was born of a peasant girl, swaddled in grave clothes and laid in a cattle feeding trough. Hopefully every believer is well past God's introduction of His Son to the world and understands God's subsequent declaration after Christ's as- cension to heaven: *"Thy throne, O God, is forever and ever; a scepter of righteousness is the scepter of Your kingdom"* (Heb. 1:8, NKJV). He is "the King of Glory" – "The Lord of Hosts" (Ps. 24:7-10).

The writer of Hebrews declares, *"He [Christ] hath by inheritance obtained a more excellent name than they [the angels]"* (Heb. 1:4). His acquired positional glory demands our respect. Seeing that Christ's exalted station in heaven is as great as His name, shall we ignore such monumental realities through careless speech? God forbid. Not only is God insulted, but diminished appreciation for Christ results in spiritual stagnation (Heb. 5:12-6:1).

In his book *The Honour of His Name*, Sir Robert Anderson extends another reason for consistently using "Lord" when speaking of Jesus Christ– it is a testimony to the unsaved:

> No one who, with open mind, has followed this inquiry respecting the use of the Lord's personal name in the New Testament, can resist the conclusion to which it leads. "The modern familiar use of the simple name 'Jesus' has NO authority in Apostolic usage." Some Christians who recognize that the common practice is unscriptural and wrong, adopt what may be described as the compromise of always adding "Christ" to the simple name." Their motive is most praiseworthy, but we do well to consider not merely what depth of meaning "Jesus Christ" may have with those who use it thus, but what it means to the vast majority of people who hear or read their words. The infidel uses it as freely as the Christian. And even with ordinary Christians, hallowed though it be, and redolent of holy memories, it is regarded (like "Jesus") as merely a personal name; and it points, not upward to the Lord of Glory on the eternal throne, but back to "the historic Jesus." [3]

The title, the Lord Jesus Christ, endorses far more theological truth than just referring to the man "Jesus" or to the Anointed One (the Christ) of God. When one speaks of the Lord Jesus Christ, one affirms the Lord Jesus' deity, rule, and position over all things. A believer, who truly loves the Lord Jesus and has yielded to His Lordship, will naturally speak of Jesus Christ as

Lord. *"If any man love not the Lord Jesus Christ, let him be Anathema"* (1 Cor. 16:22).

Ignorance of divine truth, or the rejection of it, will be evident in the absence of ascribed exaltation to the Lord Jesus Christ in our speech. If an individual only prays "sweet Jesus this" and "precious Jesus that," but never speaks of Jesus as Lord – there is a spiritual problem! The Holy Spirit enables the human will to readily proclaim Jesus Christ as Lord. Paul explains, *"Wherefore I give you to understand, that no man speaking by the Spirit of God calleth Jesus accursed: and that no man can say that Jesus is the Lord, but by the Holy Ghost [Spirit]"* (1 Cor. 12:3). The title dichotomy between "the Lord Jesus Christ" and "Jesus Christ" spans from Christ's lowly sojourn on earth to His revered seat of authority at the right hand of majesty on High.

It is understood that not everyone who speaks of Jesus Christ necessarily identifies with His Lordship – for an individual's conduct will manifest the reality of Christ within him or her (Matt. 7:21). Adolf Hilter, one of the most notable liars in human history, once pretentiously declared, "Anyone who dares to lay hands on the highest image of the Lord commits sacrilege against the benevolent Creator...."[4] Though the statement is true, his appalling exploits proved his disdain for the Lord Jesus Christ. Even the sacred text of Islam, the Quran (Koran), refers to Jesus Christ, but yet denies His deity and lordship:

> O People of the Book! Commit no excesses in your religion: Nor say of Allah aught but the truth. **Christ Jesus the son of Mary was no more than a messenger of Allah**, and His Word, which He bestowed on Mary, and a spirit proceeding from Him: so believe in Allah and His messengers. Say not 'Trinity': desist: it will be better for you: for Allah is one Allah..." (Surah 4:171)

61

A number of years ago, I regularly concluded my prayers with the nearly mechanical utterance "in Jesus name – Amen." An older and wiser brother in the Lord exhorted me in front of others to extend the Lord His full due when addressing Him. At first, I was stunned and offended, but later, I realized that my response confirmed a wrong heart-attitude – I was more concerned about my reputation than honouring the Lord. Since that time, I have endeavored to always combine an appropriate title of exaltation or honorary speech when speaking His name. This practice serves as a reminder that every time I utter His sweet name I acknowledge that He is on the throne and that I am His subject.

I am not saying that the Lord's instruction to His disciples to "pray in My name" is a mandate for some formula in prayer in which we always conclude our praying in rote, such as "in the name of the Lord Jesus Christ, Amen." Rather, we should be sensitive in using the name of Jesus casually anytime, especially while praying. "Christ," as Augustine rightly asserts, "is not valued at all unless He be valued above all." May we use every opportunity to keep the Lord enthroned in our hearts and minds. This was clearly the practice of the apostles in penning the oracles of God, as inspired by the Holy Spirit. Truly His name is above all names, so why not make all men aware of it now!

Son of Man and Son of God

The four Gospels present the Lord Jesus Christ to mankind in the only dignified manner endorsed by God. In tracing those brief years of His earthly sojourn, each Gospel writer upholds a specific viewpoint of the Saviour, thus, exposing various inherent glories for our appreciation, reverence and remembrance. It is to be understood that the books of Matthew, Mark, Luke and John are not a harmonizing attempt to portray the life of Christ but four inexhaustible and unique themes of His person and attributes. J. G. Bellett highlights the unique vantage points of the four Gospels in relationship to revealing the glory of Christ:

> And as to the ways of the blessed Lord which are, in this variety, given to us, I need not say that all is perfection. Whether it be this path or that which He takes before us – whatever relationship He sustains – whatever affection fills His soul – though different, all is perfect. He may pass before us in the conscious elevation of the Son of God, or in the sympathies of the Son of man; we may see Him in Jewish connection, in St. Matthew; or more widely abroad, as among men, in St. Luke; as the Servant of the varied need of sinners, in St. Mark; or as the solitary Stranger from heaven, in St. John; still, all is perfection. And to discern and trace this, is at once the disciple's profit and delight. *"Thy testimonies are wonderful; therefore doth my soul keep them."*[5]

"The Son of Man" is an Old Testament term, used widely in the book of Ezekiel, to express human association and, thus, links Christ to earth as a man (Dan. 7:13). Luke applies the title to the Lord Jesus twenty-five times in his Gospel, while, in contrast, John, whose theme is the deity of Christ, only refers to the Lord as the Son of Man twelve times. The Lord Jesus spoke of Himself as "the Son of Man" more often than as "the Son of God," for the divine title identified His mission and not His divine essence. It is noted that only the Lord Jesus spoke of Himself as "the Son of Man" in the Gospels, some eighty-four times; yet, fourteen references speak of "others" identifying the Lord Jesus as the "Son of God," a title He applied to Himself only five times (All of these occurrences are rightly placed in John.). The Lord normally spoke of His humble station and ministry, while others were privileged to acknowledge His divine rule and essence.

Once of the early biblical references to the "Son of Man" is found in Psalm 8. This Psalm is then quoted in the Epistle to the

Hebrews and is applied of the incarnation of Christ. The title "Son of Man" is not found in any New Testament epistle except for the one reference in Hebrew 2:6-9, which refers to Psalm 8. The Epistles inform the Church of her heavenly, not earthly, calling in Christ. The Lord Jesus will always be a man, but now He is highly exalted and at the right hand of God in heaven.

In application, it is appropriate for us to consider and ponder His humility in being the Son of Man who descended out of heaven to become the Man of Sorrows for the suffering of death. However, the reality of the matter is that He is no longer in the grave, but in fact has been exalted over all powers and authorities. For this cause, it does not seem fitting for the believer to now address Him personally as the "Son of Man." In my opinion, this is why the expression is not found in the epistles, except for the one reference in Hebrews, which explains that the Lord's incarnation was for the purpose of suffering death. Christ finished that mission to earth, and consequently, at the pleasure of the Father, He now possesses a name above all names. Sir Robert Anderson adds to this further explanation of the title "Son of Man":

> Christians are apt to treat this phrase as merely an oriental-ism for "man." But, as the Book of Daniel teaches us, it was a Divine title. And that the Jews so regarded it is clear; for the Lord's assumption of it when before the Council led them all to exclaim, *"Art thou then the Son of God?"* (Luke 22:69, 70). It is never used in Scripture in connection with the Incarnation. As man He was born in Bethlehem; but as Son of Man He *"descended out of heaven."* [6]

Only in the Acts do we read of the title "Son of Man" being uttered through mere human lips – it is Stephen's announcement to the Pharisees of what He saw in heaven just before he was martyred:

He, being full of the Holy Ghost [Spirit], looked up steadfastly into heaven, and saw the glory of God, and Jesus standing on the right hand of God, and said, Behold, I see the heavens opened, and the Son of Man standing on the right hand of God" (Acts 7:55-56).

Stephen is not addressing the Lord, but describing Him – this is an important distinction. But why did Stephen use the title of "Son of Man," for it is not used elsewhere in Scripture after the Lord's exaltation. Dean Alford offers the explanation to this question.

Stephen, full of the Holy Ghost, and speaking not of himself at all, but entirely by the utterance of the Spirit, repeats the very words in which (the Lord) Jesus Himself, before this same Council, had foretold His glorification (Matt. 24:64).[7]

In other words, Stephen was affirming that the same Man condemned before the Sanhedrin was now glorified in heaven. Stephen was declaring that there had been a direct fulfillment of Christ's words to them. Stephen used the term "Son of Man" because Christ had applied it to Himself before His crucifixion.

The Lord commonly used titles which referred to His yet future humbling – His mission to earth – but other than His forerunner, John the Baptist, who spoke of Him as *"the Lamb of God who taketh away the sin of the world,"* others did not speak of Christ in this way. This is not to say it is wrong to remember what the Lord did. We are commanded to, and certainly, the New Testament writers visit this matter often:

God sent forth His Son, made of a woman, made under the law, to redeem them that were under the law, that we might receive the adoption of sons (Gal. 4:4-5).

Let this mind be in you, which was also in Christ Jesus: Who, being in the form of God, thought it not robbery to be equal

> *with God: But made Himself of no reputation, and took upon Him the form of a servant, and was made in the likeness of men: And being found in fashion as a man, He humbled Himself, and became obedient unto death, even the death of the cross* (Phil. 2:5-8).

The point is that we should now approach Him as the exalted Son of God; far more has been revealed to us since He first referred to Himself as the Son of Man. On this side of Calvary, His people should not personally address Him by applying past expressions of His humiliation, which, except for John (Christ's forerunner), the Lord applied solely to Himself. The only apparent exception is when Scripture verifies that a title of humiliation has become a title of exaltation such as "Lamb." God's Lamb is prominent in Scripture, with one-fourth of all "lamb" references being found in Revelation. *"Worthy is the Lamb that was slain to receive power, and riches, and wisdom, and strength, and honour, and glory, and blessing"* (Rev. 5:12). Let us follow the example of Scripture in addressing the Lord.

Idioms and Euphemisms

The general populace is more prone to convey disdain for God's name through casually uttering idioms, euphemisms, and vain expressions than blatant forms of blasphemy. If you have children, you already know their natural tendency to find a way to circumvent known parental boundaries. Our flesh naturally wants to have its own way and opposes the things of God. Many know that it is wrong to speak the Lord's name in vain, so a means of doing so which is more casual and less offensive to their conscience is developed – thus idioms, euphemisms and vain expressions are manufactured.

Many idioms and euphemisms have become so commonplace in our modern society that most people utter them without thought to the significance of what they are saying. Before addressing specific errors, it would perhaps be helpful to review what idioms and euphemisms are.

Idioms are specialized jargon relating to a particular culture or people. If speaking through a translator to individuals of another culture, one would be wise to refrain from using idioms, because neither the translator nor the audience would be likely to understand what you mean. They would be more likely to apply a literal meaning to such idioms as "he kicked the bucket," "the apple does not fall far from the tree," or "my eyes are bigger than my stomach."

Euphemisms substitute less offensive words or terms for those which are explicit. For example, one might say "the late hours" or "autumn years" to speak of the time of life just prior to an elderly person's death. The once popular farewell expression "God be with you" is now the contraction "good bye." Many speak of the "Good Book" in lieu of the Bible.

A popular idiom, which has come to mean "something spectacular has been witnessed or some horrific event has happened," is "Oh my God!" The impulsive expression usually accompanies an unexpected event where either surprise or shock has been induced. When planes fly into buildings or some natural disaster suddenly strikes, it is often the first phrase you hear uttered in public. It is not posed as a prayer to God, nor does it acknowledge His sovereignty in the situation – it is an idle phrase which refers to God vainly. Some futilely speak of "the man upstairs" instead of the Lord Jesus Christ or will even use His initials "J. C." to create some expression of familiarity – as if referring to a boyhood pal. Some use the vain phrase "for heaven's sake" to express frustration over the state of their current affairs.

Euphemisms which vainly use the Lord's name or make light of spiritual truth abound: "goodness," "mercy" and "gracious" for "God" (e.g. "thank goodness" or "mercy me" or "for gracious' sakes"), "lordy" for "Lord," "gosh" or "golly" for "God," "darn" or "dang" for "damn," "darn it" or "dang it" for "damn it," "darnation" for "damnation," and "gee" (and variations) for "Jesus," "heck" for "hell" are to but name a few. Then there are various combinations like "gosh darn."

Early television shows generally refrained from deliberately using the Lord's name in vain, but how many times did we hear the Beaver or Wally (*On Leave it to Beaver*) say "Gee," "Jeez," or "Jee-wiz." In nearly every episode of *Gomer Pyle,* we heard Gomer holler out an extended "Golly." A perplexed Goofy in the Disney cartoons regularly vocalized the euphemism for "God" – "Gosh." It only took a few years for Hollywood to transition from the more culturally acceptable euphemisms to deliberate profanity and blasphemy of God's name.

Our Father which art in heaven, hallowed be Thy name (Matt. 6:9).

That at the name of Jesus every knee should bow, of things in heaven, and things in earth, and things under the earth; and that every tongue should confess that Jesus Christ is Lord, to the glory of God the Father (Phil. 2:10-11).

God, His name, His dwelling place, and His beloved Son transcend all that is common and earthly. The Lord is Holy! All that is associated with Him is to be revered. Let us magnify the name of the Lord Jesus Christ and ascribe to Him full honour and cease from casually addressing Him and vainly referring to Him.

Another Jesus

Disregard for the third of the Ten Commandments eventually results in the violation of the first and the second of the Ten Commandments. The second commandment forbids the creation of images and likenesses which could be worshipped. Dishonour of God's name disdains God Himself and allows the reprobate human mind to create a god of personal choice – one which will not condemn certain sinful behaviours or condone scriptural practices. The ideal god, an altered Jesus Christ, can then be readily embraced and worshipped as an individual determines best. The end result is that the Lord Jesus Christ has been replaced with a counterfeit god – a self-concocted phony.

Henry Morris speaks of this self-created "other Jesus":

"Jesus" is quite popular among worldly people today, but not the *true* Jesus. The popular Jesus may be the baby Jesus in the manger at Christmastime, or the buddy Jesus of Nashville "gospel" music, or the success-counseling Jesus of the positive thinkers. He may be the romantic Jesus of the Christian crooners, the rhythmic Jesus of Christian rock, or the reforming Jesus of the liberals, but none of these are the Jesus preached by the Apostle Paul, and therefore not the *real* Jesus who saves men and women from their sins.

Jesus, in reality, is the Lord Jesus Christ, the offended Creator of the universe, who had to die as man on the cross to redeem us through His shed blood, and who then rose from the dead to be set "far above all principality, and power, and might, and dominion, and every name that is named." Finally, it is *this* Jesus "who shall judge the quick and the dead at His appearing and His kingdom."

The Lord Jesus, as He really is, is not the popular Jesus of T-shirts and bumper stickers, politicians and entertainers. He was "despised and rejected of men," so they "crucified the

69

Lord of glory." He is the mighty God, the perfect Man, the only Saviour, the eternal King, and Lord of Lords. God-called teachers will not preach an imaginary Jesus who appeals to the flesh, but rather, the true Christ of creation and salvation.[8]

On one particular occasion the Lord asked His disciples an exceedingly significant question, *"Who do you say that I am?"* (Matt 16:15, NKJV). Without any hesitation Peter responded, *"You are the Christ, the Son of the living God"* (Matt. 16:16, NKJV). Dear reader, who do you say that Christ is? Is He the Lord Jesus Christ or another Jesus?

Lord Jesus, We Love Thee

Lord Jesus, we love Thee, and joyfully pour
    Our praise and our worship at They blessed feet;
Lord Jesus, we honor, exalt and adore
    The name that to God and to us is so sweet.
Thy name, blessed Lord, is as ointment poured forth
    And, even as we breathe it, its fragrance doth rise.
Thou only, blest Father, its excellent worth
    Its matchless perfection and fullness can prize.
O, name of good savor, of peace and of rest –
    The name of the Victim, the Lamb that was slain!
O, name of God's loved One in Whom we are blest!
    Oh, name ever worthy all homage to gain!
Blest Lord, in Thy name would we boast all day long,
    And praise till we reach Thee on heaven's bright shore;
Thou shalt be forever our joy and our song;
    Lord Jesus, we praise Thee, we love and adore.

– C. H. Von Poseck

The Lord of Titles

Several years ago, I was asked to give the commencement address at a graduation ceremony for a homeschooling organization. It was quite an affair with speeches, skits and music performances. Several hundred people would be in attendance. As the big "to-do" drew near, I was contacted by the individual responsible for the program bulletin. She confirmed the time allotted for the message and wanted to verify the title that was to be placed by my name on the program. I said, "Just put my name and nothing else." She responded, "Everyone has a title that has a key part in the program. Don't you have a title?" My response to her went something like this, "No, please just put 'Mr. Warren Henderson.' I am not a 'Reverend' or 'Holy ...' as these titles are reserved for the Lord alone. Besides there is no example of a disciple of Christ anywhere in Scripture having a title of position before his or her name, for all such titles are reserved for Christ." When the bulletins were passed out the night of the ceremony, I observed that I was the only individual in the program who did not have a title. How men love titles.

Though no disciple of Christ had any title before his or her name, the Lord Jesus, as previously shown, had plenty of titles, with "Lord" and "Christ" being the predominant associations. In Revelation 22:21, the last verse in the Bible, John writes of the "Lord Jesus Christ;" thus, the Bible concludes with the revelation and veneration of the Lord Jesus Christ, the Son of God and the Saviour of the world.

Men covet titles so that they might be honoured by others – it is a natural pull of our fallen nature. But those who worship Christ must not dishonour Him by stealing His glory. Listen to the solemn words of the Lord Jesus on this very matter:

> But be not ye called Rabbi: for one is your Master, even Christ; and all ye are brethren. And call no man your father upon the earth: for one is your Father, which is in heaven. Neither be ye called masters: for one is your Master, even Christ. But he that is greatest among you shall be your servant. And whosoever shall exalt himself shall be abased; and he that shall humble himself shall be exalted (Matt. 23:8-12).

Disciples of Christ do not seek the praise of men or titles of position before their names – all titles of status and all praise are reserved for the Lord Jesus Christ. John the baptizer, speaking of Christ, declared the proper obligation of all true believers: *"He must increase, but I must decrease"* (John 3:30).

> Let me not, I pray you, accept any man's person, **neither let me give flattering titles unto man**. For I know not to give flattering titles; in so doing my Maker would soon take me away (Job 32:21-22)

Many of the common expressions we use to refer to each other or to individuals in Scripture do not conform to the same scriptural etiquette upheld by the Holy Spirit in conveying honour to the Lord. For example, we do not read of "Doctor Luke," but "Luke, the beloved physician." Nor do we read of "the Apostle Paul" but "Paul an apostle of Jesus Christ." No titles of position are found before any disciples' names in Scripture. No "Saint Matthew," no "Elder Peter," no Pastor ..., no Minister ..., no Deacon.... Men love titles, yet Scripture provides none, except for the Lord Jesus Christ – All titles of position belong to

Him. As a side note, terms of association or endearment relating to believers, such as "brother" or "sister," are permitted: Paul is referred to as "brother Paul" (Acts 9:17; 22:13; 2 Pet. 3:15), Apollos as "brother Apollos" (1 Cor. 16:12), and Timothy is spoken of as "brother Timothy" in Hebrews 13:23.

How we address the Lord and others does matter. May each of us esteem the Lord more and human titles less. His name is Holy, and only He is to be revered and reverenced by men.

Church Leadership Offices or Titles?

The New Testament reveals ministries and offices for believers, but no titles. There were apostles, elders, deacons, evangelists, pastor-teachers, etc., but no disciple of Christ was referred to by a title before his name. It has been the practice of the church for centuries, however, to ascribe to men titles that they ought not to have. One of the most prevalent is the title "Pastor" as applied to the individual leader of a local church. First of all, no example of one man overseeing any local church may be found in the New Testament, except for perhaps proud heavy-handed Diotrephes who loved the preeminence and did evil in the sight of God (3 Jn. 9-11). The New Testament pattern clearly points to a plurality of shared leadership. Normally these men were referred to as "elders."

Acts 15:6, 22	Elders in the church at Jerusalem.
James 5:14	Elders to be called for healing the sick.
Acts 14:23	Paul and Barnabas recognized "elders in every church."
1 Peter 5:1	"The elders among you."

Titus 1:5   Paul instructed Titus to appoint elders in every city (church).

Acts 20:17, 28   Elders were among the church at Ephesus.

Philippians 1:1   Paul addressed the elders (bishops) and deacons of the church.

The elders had equal authority, but not necessarily equal gift or the same gift – this difference is what gives church leadership strength and balance. The New Testament mainly applies three Greek words (including verb forms) in association with those in local church leadership: *presbuteros*, *episkopos*, and *poimen*.

The Greek word *presbuteros* is found sixty-seven times in the New Testament and is primarily translated as "elder(s)" but once as "old men." A related word *presbuterion* occurs three times and is also translated "elders," except for the reference in 1 Timothy 4:14 in which it is rendered "presbytery." Of these seventy instances, four relate to Old Testament patriarchs, twenty-nine times to the Sanhedrin, twelve to the "twenty-four elders" in Revelation, and seventeen times to New Testament church leadership. *Presbuteros* is the most common word employed to speak of those in church leadership (the office).

A second Greek word associated with church leadership is *episkopos* which occurs nine times in the New Testament (including verb form) and is the second most common word used to refer to those in church leadership. It is used to refer to Judas once and to general Christian watchfulness once, as a title of Christ once, and six times to speak of local church leadership. It is normally translated "bishop" or "overseer," speaking of the leadership role within the local church; Scripture never endorses the authority of an overseer beyond the local assembly he serves.

74

The last Greek word connected with the topic of church leadership is *poimen*. It is found eighteen times in the New Testament, and its verb form *poimaino* also occurs eleven times in the New Testament. *Poimen* is translated "shepherd" in every instance but one in which it is translated "pastors" in connection with those teaching in the church (Eph. 4:11). *Poimaino* is rendered "to feed," or "to rule." Of the combined twenty-nine instances, seventeen refer to Christ, four speak of literal shepherds, five are miscellaneous in application, and one (in the plural form) refers to those serving in pastoral care of God's sheep.

To better understand whom Christ is bestowing to the Church as a gift for her edification, a comment concerning the grammatical construction of Ephesians 4:11 is pertinent. Ephesians 4:11 reads, *"And He gave some, apostles; and some, prophets; and some, evangelists; and some, pastors and teachers."* Notice the definite article "some" before "apostles," "prophets," "evangelists," and "pastors," but there is none preceding "teachers." The Greek article is translated "some" rather than "the" in this verse because the associated nouns are plural in number. Kenneth Wuest expounds the Greek grammatical rule that applies to this verse:

> When two nouns in the same case are connected by the Greek word "and," and the first noun is preceded by the article "the," the second noun is not preceded by the article, the second noun refers to the same person or thing to which the first noun refers, and is a further description of it. For instance, the words "pastors" and "teachers" in Eph. 4:11 are in the same case and are connected by the word "and." The word "pastors," is preceded by the article "the," whereas the word "teachers" is not. This construction requires us to understand that the words "pastors" and "teachers" refer to the same individual, and that the word "teacher" is a further description of the individual

called a "pastor." The expression therefore refers to pastors who are also teachers, "teaching-pastors.[1]

Consequently, the title "Pastor" is never ascribed in any personal sense (including an *office*) to anyone in the Bible other than the Lord Jesus. He is "The Good *Poimen*" (John 10:11), "The Great *Poimen*" (Heb. 13:20), and *"The Archipoimen"* (Chief Shepherd, 1 Pet. 5:4) as well as the *Poimen* (Shepherd) of our souls (1 Pet. 2:25). No man dare add the Lord's title of "Shepherd" or "Pastor" in front of their name. Those in church leadership are to pastor (verb form) God's people out of love and submission to the Pastor, the Lord Jesus. Elder is the office, and pastoring is the *gift*, the function of the elder.

In a related topic, the term "Youth Pastor" insinuates that the God ordained leadership of the local church is somehow incapable of attending to *all the sheep* God has entrusted into their care. The elders' charge is the entire "flock" (speaking of the local assembly): Paul, speaking to the elders at Ephesus, said, *"Take heed, therefore, unto yourselves, and **to all the flock** over [among] the which the Holy Ghost [Spirit] hath made you overseers, to **feed the church** of God..."* (Acts 20:28). Peter exhorts other elders to *"**Shepherd the flock of God which is among you**, serving as overseers, not by compulsion but willingly, not for dishonest gain but eagerly; nor as being lords over those entrusted to you, but **being examples to the flock**"*(1 Pet. 5:2-3, NKJV). There is nothing wrong with an individual discipling and ministering to young people, but the concept of a title for this ministry is foreign to Scripture and breeds a generational clique within the household of God. The more all the *flock* feed together, are known to each other and are encouraged to serve one another, the more the assembly will experience a productive and joyful body life.

Besides avoiding the bestowal of titles such as "Holy," "Father," "Master," "Reverend," and "Pastor" upon men, an additional comment is warranted for the term "minister." The title "minister" is not biblically applied to those in church leadership; in fact, the term is applied in a variety of ways in the New Testament: it is spoken of as a spiritual gift (Rom. 12:7), and is applied to those in civil authority (Rom. 13:1-4), to different believers as they serve Christ in various capacities (1 Cor. 3:5, 4:1; 2 Cor. 6:4, 11:15) and to Christ, who is a minister of the truth to the Jews (Rom. 15:8). It is never used as a title before a proper name anywhere in Scripture, however. August Van Ryn comments to this truth:

> According to the Word of God every believer is a "minister" and should function as such. There are of course, godly and wise leaders among the saints and true ministers of Christ, but God's Word in no manner of form allows the taking of titles and thus setting the clergy above and in a special class from all believers. In its worst form, often, instead of such feeding the flock, they are in the business of shearing the sheep, and clothing themselves with the wool.[2]

The "pastor thinking" spills over in other terminology. For example there are half a dozen references in 1 and 2 Timothy and Titus to "teaching," and one to "evangelist," but there is not a single mention of "pastoring" or "shepherding," yet many refer to these as the "Pastoral Epistles." Clearly unbiblical presuppositions are being applied into the text to support an unscriptural form of church government. While it is true that Paul was guiding Titus and Timothy in their God-ordained ministries to local churches, there is no endorsement of a clergy position within these texts.

Often those individuals ordained by human designation as able church leaders are referred to as clergy. The English word "clergy" comes from the Greek word *kleros*, which means a "lot." In the New Testament, *kleros* is translated: "heritage," "inheritance," "lot," and "part." It is used in Acts 1:17 and 25 to describe the method (casting lots, see Acts 1:26) which was used to determine who would be the replacement apostle (This practice was not decreed by God.). In summary, *kleros* could mean the lot itself or the portion obtained through the lot. After the ascension of Christ, Matthias was selected as a replacement apostle by lot. Eventually, the term *kleros* came to mean the person selected for the ministerial office – whether or not selected by lot. It is noted that the English word "laity" comes from the Greek word *laos*, which simply means "people."

The much debated verse is 1 Peter 5:3: *"Neither as being lords over God's **heritage**, but being examples to the flock."* The Greek word *kleros* is translated "heritage" in this verse. Peter is speaking to fellow elders (*presbuteros*); thus, some have argued that church leaders have a rightful church position of "clergy." However, other Bible translations more clearly confirm who the "heritage" is: *"those entrusted to you"* (NKJV), *"those allotted to your charge"* (NASV), *"the charge allotted to you"* (RV). Wuest's Expanded Translation renders it: "the portions of the flock assigned to you."[3] *Vine's Expository Dictionary* states that *Kleros* in 1 Peter 5:3 speaks of those assigned to the spiritual care of elders. The dictionary then notes, "From *kleros* the word 'clergy' is derived (**a transposition in the application of the term**)."[4] Clearly the *kleros* of 1 Peter 5:3 is not those shepherding God's flock, but the portion of the flock which is in their care.

Harry A. Ironside summarizes this whole matter concisely:

Note the expression, 'the elders which are among you.' There is no suggestion here of a clerical order ruling arbitrarily over the laity. These elders were mature, godly men, upon whom rested the responsibility of watching over the souls of believers, as those for whom they must give an account (Heb. 13:17).[5]

For approximately the first 150 years of the Church Age, the New Testament model of church leadership was followed, but then men created positions and hierarchies which squelched church body life, oppressed the saints of God, and began the makings of Roman Catholicism. The clerical system since that time has oppressed the ministry of believer-priests, and the church seems to be satisfied to let it be so. J. I. Packer summarized the matter in concise and blunt language:

> By clericalism I mean that combination of conspiracy and tyranny to which the minister claims, and the congregation agrees, that all spiritual ministry is his responsibility and not theirs: a notion that is both disreputable in principle and Spirit quenching in the practice.[6]

Erwin W. Lutzer also candidly describes the spiritually stagnating effect that the clerical system has had on the body of Christ:

> The word *layman* has crept into our vocabulary to describe the laity, that is, the vast majority of Christians who do not belong to the "professional" ministry known as the clergy. The use of this distinction has crippled the impact of the church on the world. Thousands of Christians have shirked their God-given responsibilities because they expect their pastor, minister, or priest (or whatever designation their church adopts) to perform all spiritual functions. The minister is expected to execute his duties so well that the people need not have any meaningful involvement in the church of Jesus Christ. The more competent the minister, the better, so that fewer requirements fall on the shoulders of the congregation.[7]

The Lord Himself issued a grave warning to those who seized the rule over His people: *"the deeds of the Nicolaitans, which I also hate"* (Rev. 2:6) and *"the doctrine of the Nicolaitans, which thing I hate"* (Rev. 2:15). "Nicolaitans" means "rule over the laity." *Thayer's Greek Lexicon* provides this meaning of *Nicolaitans*: "destruction of the people."[8] A ruling body of clergy had evidently conquered the people, and they are still conquering today. The only position of hierarchy in the Church is to be Christ the head over the body. Those in church leadership have a ministry to the Chief Shepherd, not an elevated position above fellow believers. Whatever authority the elders have springs forth from lives of godliness and subjection to the Lord, not human ambition, certificates or titles. *"Not he that commendeth himself is approved, but whom the Lord commendeth"* (2 Cor. 10:18).

The first two chapters of Revelation provide an important example of what happens when the Church's affection for its Head – Christ – wanes. In order of digression, the church at Ephesus left its first love – Christ (Rev. 2:4), as a result *"the deeds of the Nicolaitans"* (Rev. 2:6) developed in that church, which then led to *"the doctrine of the Nicolaitans"* in the church at Pergamum (Rev. 2:15). With Christ supplanted as head by a clergy system, the next compromise was that a woman named Jezebel was being allowed to teach and lead the church at Thyatira (Rev. 2:20). Following next is the church at Sardis, unto whom the Lord says, *"thou hast a name that thou livest, and art dead"* (Rev. 3:1). The Church engages in dead works when Christ is not the center and head of its gathering. Six times the Lord demands that these four churches repent of their wicked ways. The Lord is the Head of the Church, and He has put the Church under a specific order to ensure that He will always be honoured. Straying from this order ensures His disproval and the Church's spiritual downfall.

It goes without saying that the majority of Christendom is ascribing inappropriate titles to men, and worse yet, most of these titles are ones which are reserved for the Lord Jesus alone. Let us not demean Christ by robbing Him of His position and affording it to another or by applying exalted titles to those who should know better. Exodus 30:37-38 extends to us an Old Testament picture of the reverence we are to have for God and for those things which pertain to Him and Him alone.

> *And as for the perfume which thou shalt make, ye shall not make to yourselves according to the composition thereof: it shall be unto thee holy for the Lord. Whosoever shall make like unto that, to smell thereto, shall even be cut off from his people* (Ex. 30:37-38).

The incense to be burned upon the Golden Altar in the tabernacle during daily offerings was for God's appreciation alone. Man was prohibited from combining the offering spices in any form for his own personal enjoyment – it was to be offered to the Lord; no man was to enjoy and appreciate its fragrance. Let man not steal from God what titles He has declared are His alone!

The Lord of Gatherings

Leighton Ford, the brother-in-law of Billy Graham, once wrote "Our whole vocabulary of church activity will change if we really begin to take seriously the New Testament pattern."[1] The Church's trek through time has proven her propensity to embrace unbiblical terminology and religious phraseology in doctrine and practice. These often erroneous expressions are common in our speech, in our singing and in our prayers. The simple fact of the matter is that unscriptural talk leads to unbiblical practices in time. As the Church is under Christ's authority, meets in His name, and gathers in His presence we do not want to employ errant terminology and practices which would supplant Christ's rule as Head of the Church – He is Lord of all gatherings of the Church.

For example, sometimes we hear a brother praying to the Holy Spirit to anoint a particular speaker, but no such prayer is found in Scripture. The Holy Spirit does commune with the believer (2 Cor. 13:14), for His very residence conveys to our spirit thoughts of adoption and sonship (Rom. 8:15), and comfort for the soul (John 14:16). But we do not pray to the Holy Spirit for the Lord Jesus Christ is the only Mediator between God and Man (1 Tim. 2:5). The Holy Spirit will, on His own initiative, intercede with Christ on our behalf when we know not what to pray (Rom. 8:26).

Secondly, the spiritual anointing received by a believer at conversion is spoken of as a one time event with enduring results

(1 Jn. 2:20, 27). Do such prayers teach our children to expect a future *anointing* of the Holy Spirit, when Scripture does not identify such? There is to be ongoing Spirit-filling in the believer's life, and there are those mysterious experiences in which God's favor is wondrously dispensed to certain believers to uniquely equip them for ... (I will not presume to know the mind of God on this matter, nor do I know what to call these spiritual endowments), but spiritual *anointing* specifically outfits the believer to discern truth from error (1 Jn. 2:27).

Paul exhorted the Christians at Philippi to *"prove* [or distinguish] *the things that differ"* (Phil. 1:10, R.V.). Wuest's expanded translation puts it this way: "recognize the true value of finer distinctions involved in Christian conduct and then sanctify them."[2] In this chapter, we will review the things which differ in relationship to what may distract the Lord's people from upholding the headship of Christ in the meetings of the Church.

The doctrines of men often develop from carelessly dividing God's Word, or through the complacency of not correcting what is known to be not quite right. Often these matters are only slight distortions in truth and really don't arouse much attention until after the harm is realized. Satan rarely presents outright lies; rather, he depends upon a series of blurred deceptions to gain His footing and to wreak havoc within the Church. I will illustrate this point: "Despite what you might have thought previously, *black* really means *white.*" You say, "No, black is the opposite of white." But then I pick up a reliable dictionary, say *The American Heritage Dictionary*[3]*,* and show you that the meaning of "black" is "dark," and then I confirm that one of the meanings of "dark" is "dim." Finding the entry for "dim" I prove to you that "dim" can mean "pale." And finally I look up the word "pale" and verify that one of the meanings of "pale" is "white." I have proven to you using a series of only four imprecise meanings, (variations of the best meaning, if you will) that *black* is equal to *white.*

Religious Symbols

Men love religious symbols, figures and traditions to improve their pious experience, but all that is not biblically instituted will tend, in time, to detract and distract from the work and person of Jesus Christ. There are only three symbolic practices commanded of the Church: the head covering to show visible agreement with God's creation order (1 Cor. 11:2-16), the Lord's Supper in which the bread and wine are to remind believers of the broken body and shed blood of Christ at Calvary (1 Cor. 11:17-33), and water baptism which provides public identification with Christ in obedience of His command (Matt. 28:19-20) – the identification truths of a believer dying with Christ and being made alive with Him are illustrated in water baptism (Rom. 6:3-6). There were no other symbols or metaphoric practices extended to the Church by Scripture, except, perhaps in James 5 where church elders were to anoint a believer with oil to symbolize the healing God provides, especially to those who had been suffering because of unrepentant personal sin, but now were taking sides with God against themselves on the matter.

So how did the church ever incorporate crosses, denominational symbols, pictures of dead saints, and religious flags into its doings and gatherings? Satan, the great mimicker of God, often takes expression and symbols from the Bible and ascribes new meanings to them. For example: the rainbow has been used to symbolize the New Age teaching of man's transition into the Aquarian age (his journey to deity), and the term "born again" is used by many to describe reincarnation or spiritual rededication. There will be attempts by the devil to distort the true scriptural meaning of biblical symbols or to construct new symbols to distract Christians from scriptural teaching. The cross may be a good reminder of Christ, but how often the cross itself is sung about and worshipped. The cross was the instrument of shame and suffering; the Lord who hung upon it is to be the focus of our attention.

Pulling Judaism into Christianity

There is a proclivity of men to create visual stimulus to accentuate their religious experience. Many of the religious symbols that the Church has manufactured are simply Old Testament *figures* of what now is reality in Christ. Judaism was full of future-related imagery which appealed to the senses, whereas Christianity is spiritual and only appreciated by faith, not our natural senses. Christ has come and, therefore, replaced all the types and shadows which were the prelude of the spiritual realities and good things to come (Heb. 8:13). So how is Judaism intruding into the gatherings of the Church? Here are a few examples.

Robes and Candles

The Jewish priests had ephods, and much of the *clergy* in Christendom today wear spectacular colored robes. The Jewish priests burned incense and trimmed a lighted lampstand in the tabernacle. Many in Christendom light candles and wave incense canisters to mimic the religious practices of old.

The Sanctuary

The "sanctuary" in the Old Testament referred to a location within the temple or tabernacle where the priests officiated in worship on behalf of the nation of Israel. In the New Testament, it is never applied to a physical room in which the Church gathers for worship. In the Old Testament, access to God was limited. Only the High Priest could gain entry into the Most Holy Place of the tabernacle and temple, and he did so in trepidation and not without the blood of a goat and bullock. Through Christ's work at Calvary, the inner veil was rent from top to bottom to illustrate that through Christ God could have full fellowship with man and man could have full access to God.

So all those "Sanctuary" signs we see in church buildings should really be turned to point up instead of down the hallway, or one might wrap a string about the sign and choose to wear it over one's head so it points to themself – for God dwells within those who have been born again during the Church Age (1 Cor. 6:19), and therefore also within a local assembly (1 Cor. 3:16-17). No bricks and mortar can contain Him, but those who have responded to His invitation to be saved have His abiding presence forever.

The Altar

Some call the wooden table in front of the "sanctuary" (an already explained misnomer) a *prayer altar*. Concerning altars, the Church has none but Christ (Heb. 13:10), and He is in heaven. How demeaning it is to Christ to ascribe His ministry in heaven to a piece of manmade furniture! Some bow the knee before such religious objects to extend artificial reverence to God. Through Christ and Him alone is the believer's worship offered to God. Using terms such as "prayer altar" or "altar calls" simply shows one's ignorance of God's dispensational economies revealed in Scripture.

Since the first man walked upon the earth, God has been proving His greatness and man's inclination to fail in his godly stewardship in order to emphasize that salvation is only received by divine grace through faith. Ignorance of dispensational theology allows Judaism to ever so gently creep into Christian practices and effectually mars the clear testimony of Christ. Let us not be bowing down to pieces of furniture in the guise of being religious; if it supplants Christ, it is an idol!

The House of God

The term "house of God" occurs ninety times in the Bible, with eighty-seven of those occurrences speaking of the Old Testament reality of God's dwelling place among His people in a tent or a temple. All three references to "the house of God" in the Epistles refer to the Church. During the Church Age, God dwells in His people, not a building (1 Cor. 6:19-20). *"But if I tarry long, that thou mayest know how thou oughtest to behave thyself in* **the house of God, which is the church** *of the living God, the pillar and ground of the truth"* (1 Tim. 3:15). The "house of God" is not a building, but a *household* of God's people. The NASB actually renders the expression *"house of God"* in this verse as *"household of God."* Wrong terminology introduces an alternate idea of what the Church is, which is not biblical. The Church is not a dead building; it is a living body. So the next time someone welcomes you to "the house of God" (speaking of the building), you might ask them "Through what door does one gain entrance into the house of God?" The answer is the Lord Jesus (John 10:1; 14:6). He is the only spiritual entrance into the spiritual house called the Church (Eph. 2:19-22).

Lord's Supper or the Communion Service?

The Lord Jesus instituted the "Lord's Supper" as a time for corporate remembrance for the local church (1 Cor. 11:17, 20). He said to do it often, understanding our tendency to forget Him and His work. Yet the command set down no rules for how frequently Christians should gather to remember the Lord; our love for Him will determine this matter. The early church transitioned from "breaking bread" daily in Acts 2 to the established pattern of remembering the Lord once a week on Sunday (Acts 20:7). Every believer should confess their sins before partaking of the Lord's Supper (1 Cor. 11:23-32), just as the Levitical priests washed their hands and feet at the bronze laver before entering into the tabernacle to burn incense before the Lord (Ex. 30:17-21). If a Levitical priest did not prepare properly to offer worship, he was in danger of dying. Paul acknowledges that the Christian, a believer priest (1 Pet. 2:5, 9) faces the same peril at the Lord's Supper, if he or she approaches God to take the bread and wine with unconfessed sin. God has appointed a specific way for the Church to uplift the name of His Son and remember Him in the corporate setting – the Lord's Supper.

When believers assemble for the Lord's Supper, they should do so in the beauty of holiness (sins humbly confessed) and with a spiritual offering ready to present to the Lord (1 Chron. 16:29). As in all the meetings of the Church, the audible ministry should be done by Spirit-led men, as the man represents God when speaking (1 Cor. 11:7) and according to the speaking instructions given for church order (1 Cor. 14:26-35). The women should attend to the visual ministry in the assembly of revealing God's glory by covering all competing glories (herself being man's glory and her hair which is her glory – 1 Cor. 11:7, 15). In this way, only God's glory, as represented by uncovered men, is seen by God and the angels overlooking the assembly – a visible salute to Christ's headship and God's order is affirmed for all to see. This pictures the scene in heaven as seraphim and cherubim cover their own intrinsic glories with their wings in the presence of God, so only God's glory is preeminent (Isa. 6:2; Ezek. 1:11).

Often the biblical term "the Lord's Table" (speaking of a spiritual table in which we receive blessing and fellowship in Christ – 1 Corinthians 10) is confused with the biblical term "the Lord's Supper" (the remembrance meeting of the local church spoken of in 1 Corinthians 11). Consequently, most of Christendom refers to the Lord's Supper by the unscriptural term "the communion service." There is *communion with Christ* at the Lord's Table, but more specifically, there is a *remembrance of*

Christ at every Lord's Supper – the value of His death is to be proclaimed afresh.

The Lord's Table speaks to the sum total of the spiritual blessings we have in Christ, while the Lord's Supper refers to the remembrance meeting of the Church. In the sense that the souls of believers are refreshed through Spirit-led worship, the Lord's Table probably includes the Lord's Supper, but the distinction of terminology and significance of each should not be lost. It is a great privilege to remember and refresh the Saviour during the Lord's Supper and also a blessing to the heart of every believer to commune with and partake of the Saviour at His Table. Appendix B summarizes the similarities and differences of the Lord's Table and the Lord's Supper.

Applying the wrong terminology of "Communion Service" to "Lord's Supper" effectively exchanges the purpose of the meeting. At the Lord's Supper we are to give unto the Lord, rather than expect to be served by Him. The word "service" conveys an entirely different intention of the Lord's Supper than what Scripture conveys. The Communion Service terminology also undermines the seriousness of the matter of departing from "the Lord's Table" to spiritually eat (partake) of "the table of demons." Clearly the Church will leave the table that is set at the remembrance meeting, but not "The Lord's Table." In consequence, the term "Communion Service" diminishes the remembrance focus of Christ at the Lord's Supper and undermines the significance of His ongoing fellowship at "The Lord's Table."

Worship Leaders

Contemporary terms such as "Worship Team," "Worship Pastor" and "Worship Leaders" have crept into many church gatherings. Are these terms found in Scripture? The answer is "no." In fact the concept is foreign to Scripture. If there is any "Worship Leader" in the local assembly, it is the Holy Spirit. His role is to guide believers into a deeper understanding of truth concerning the Lord Jesus and the overall greatness and goodness of God. Only through Spirit-led worship, which will be completely founded in divine truth, can the believer offer any acceptable sacrifice of praise unto God.

But the hour cometh, and now is, when the true worshippers shall worship the Father in spirit and in truth: for the Father seeketh such to worship Him. God is a Spirit: and they that worship Him must worship Him in spirit and in truth (John 4:23-24).

Howbeit when He, the Spirit of truth, is come, He will guide you into all truth: for He shall not speak of Himself; but whatsoever He shall hear, that shall He speak: and He will show you things to come. He shall glorify Me: for He shall receive of Mine, and shall show it unto you (John 16:13-14).

Reviewing how the word "worship" is used in Scripture provides helpful insights into what God expects from those He created for His good pleasure. *Vine's Expository Dictionary of Biblical Words* shows the following Greek words rendered *worship* and their associated meanings.[4] The number of times a particular Greek word occurs in the New Testament (by its type of speech) is shown below alongside the word's associated meaning.

Worship (verbs)

Word	Meaning	Occurrences
Proskuneo	to make obeisance, do reverence to	60
Sebomai	to revere	10
Sebazomai	to honour religiously	1
Latreuo	to serve, to render religious service	21
Eusebeo	to act piously towards	2
	Total	94

Worship (nouns)

Word	Meaning	Occurrences
Sebasma	an object of worship	2
Ethelothreskeia	"will-worship" (voluntary worship)	4
Threskeia:	"Religion" (a ceremonial observance)	1
	Total	7

Probing beyond the meanings of worship, to the context of these seven instances in which the noun form of worship is used, we find that believer's worship is not the focus; in fact most references are negative in connotation (i.e. relating to false worship or man's religious rote):

Acts 17:23 speaks of idol worship.

2 Thessalonians 2:4 relates to the anti-Christ during the Tribulation period.

Acts 26:5 speaks of the religious sect of the Pharisees.

Colossians 2:18 faults the worship of angels.

James 1:26 talks of man's religion.

James 1:27 clarifies what "pure religion" is in the form of a test.

Colossians 2:23 addresses legalism as religious showmanship.

As there are no adjectives to evaluate, and the above nouns do not relate directly to the believer's worship, we are left with an abundance of verbs confirming that "worship" is something that we do; it does not describe what we have done for God, nor does it describe who we are! So the entire concept of someone standing up before a congregation of the Lord's people as a "worship leader" is unknown in Scripture. As a believer priest, all Christians are to be worshipping God, and the Holy Spirit will guide and lead the activity. Introducing worship as an adjective or to formulate a title for men is opposed to the clear usage of the word in Scripture.

In light of how "worship" is spoken of in Scripture, it must be concluded that referring to the Lord's Supper as the "worship meeting" is not actually correct. It is not to say that worship doesn't happen during this meeting, or for that matter, at any other meeting of the Church. Certainly, God's people in the Old Testament worshipped God while Ezra was teaching them from the Scripture (Neh. 8:1-8). The Lord's Supper is an appointed time for the local church to remember the Lord Jesus and to proclaim the value of His death (1 Cor. 11:24-26). It is a remembrance meeting in which the Lord's people will certainly worship the Lord, but it is more specific than a *worship meeting*. The danger of the change in terminology is that in time the *worship meeting* will become an opportunity for offering "strange fire" unto the Lord in the name of Christ, while neglecting what Christ commanded His supper to be. It has happened before, and it may happen again – we provide a higher degree of protection against drifting by adhering to the biblical intent for and the name of the meeting.

The idea of the Lord's Supper being *the worship meeting* has already influenced the conduct of some. For example, some sisters only wear a head-covering during *the worship meeting* and not at other church meetings. Why? Because in their thinking, that is the only meeting in which the assembly worships God. In fact, there should be worship, praise and adoration for the Lord at all meetings – we should never be conscious of a time when the Lord is not at the center of our attention. Some dress nicer for *the worship meeting* than at other meetings of the Church. A suit and tie for *the worship meeting* and jeans and a T-shirt at the prayer meeting. But why the difference   isn't the Lord present in all the meetings? Does not the Lord preside over all the gatherings of His people?

The reality for the believer-priest is that he or she can offer worship to God at any moment in time. Every time we yield to God's truth instead of pursuing our lusts and selfish will, we offer a living sacrifice unto God (Rom. 12:1-2). It is the pagan that works to *induce or force* worship and usually through disordered music (Dan. 3), but the Lord's people may be, and should be, prompted to worship from a joyful heart anytime, not just at one particular meeting. So let us be careful that we worship God without worshipping our worship!

The Church Service

Perhaps you have heard the story of two men chatting in the doorway of a chapel just before the church meeting was ready to begin. A stranger, approaching the two men, asked, "What time does the service begin?" One of the two men promptly replied, "As soon as the meetings are over." Most of Christianity views "church" as something you do on Sunday mornings. Many professing Christians venture once a week into a comfortably furnished building for their one hour dose of religiosity. They settle into a soft seat and enjoy the stimulation of good music and heightened self-esteem brought on by an emotionally arousing and entertaining message.

The "me first" focus of our society has deeply infiltrated the attitudes of the Church. Often I have heard someone say, "I quit going to that church because I wasn't getting anything out of it." Most of Christianity gathers on Sunday morning to *get,* not to *give.* What pathetic body life – most of the body's parts are not functioning, but rather are draining off the energy and time of others. On this point Kenneth C. Fleming writes:

The Church speaks of "service," but in reality nearly everyone is being served. The better we feel about ourselves after an hour or so, the better we think the "service" was. Only a small minority do more than sit and listen. Some feel that they have "served God" by being there, but really we have been served by the preacher or teacher. In contrast, the Lord Jesus came not to be served by to serve (Mark 10:45).[5]

As the Church engages less and less in serving others, the distinction in Scripture of "salvation" and "service" are becoming blurred – thus creating the opportunity of doctrinal error. For example, John 15:1-11 is used by some to teach you can lose your salvation, but the subject matter is service – fruit bearing. "Fruit" is mentioned eight times and the need to "abide" in Christ to be fruitful nine times. "Repentance," "faith," "believing," and "salvation" are not mentioned at all in the chapter. Christ was speaking to His disciples who needed not salvation from hell, but spiritual fruit to their accounts (Phil. 4:17). They didn't need a Saviour, they needed Christlikeness. It is a good example where wrong terminology feeds wrong interpretation of Scripture and actually promotes, what A. W. Tozer describes as, a near comatose state of spiritual existence:

> In the average *church service* the most real thing is the shadowy unreality of everything. The worshiper sits in a state of suspended *mentation*; a kind of dreamy numbness creeps upon him; he hears words, but they do not register, he cannot relate them to anything on his own life level. . . . It does not affect anything in his everyday life. He is aware of no power, no presence, no spiritual reality.[6]

1 Corinthians 3:10-15 and 9:24-27 are other passages which are commonly misunderstood because the elements of "salvation" and "service" are not correctly discerned – it is no wonder

95

the professing Church is losing the understanding of the distinction and, consequently, power in service! If my focus is to attend a church "service," I have a selfish expectation of being served; but if I go to "meet Him," I have an expectation of being refreshed by the presence of the Lord as I worship Him and serve others. Biblically speaking, the phrase "come together" is used a dozen times in the New Testament to describe local believers gathering regularly for corporate worship, prayer, teaching and fellowship (Acts 2:42). They simply *came together* in the name of Christ – there were no *church services*; the church serving began after the meetings were over.

The believer was saved to serve, not to be served. One works his way up in the kingdom of God through lowering himself in humble service to others in the name of Christ (Matt. 18:1-4; Phil. 2:1-5). The way up is down! All believers should be coming to the Lord's Supper with sins confessed and while contemplating thoughts of adoration for the Saviour (1 Cor. 11:20-32). All believers should be using their gifts and abilities to edify and build up the body of Christ (1 Cor. 12:23-26). Involvement builds commitment, so those in church leadership need to challenge and involve all those in the local assembly to take part in the care of and ministry to the local assembly. Remembering that we were created for God's good pleasure, and not to indulge our own, will be helpful in maintaining the right mindset (Rev. 4:11).

Church Nomenclature

On the day of Pentecost some 2000 years ago, the church was formed. The Holy Spirit came and baptized believers into the body of Christ (1 Cor. 1:12-13), so that there is now one universal body of Christ composed of both Jews and Gentiles (Eph. 2:14-18, Eph. 4:4). Scripture clearly speaks, however, of believers who gathered in the name of the Lord Jesus at certain locales – local churches within the universal Church (Phil 1:1, Gal. 1:2). It is noted that the large majority of references to the "church" in the New Testament speak of the local reality; this emphasizes the significance God puts upon the body life of local gatherings.

The Universal Church:

All true believers are redeemed and compose the body of Christ:

There is no distinction of gender, social class, wealth, or ethnic heritage (Gal. 3:28; 1 Cor. 12:13).

Christ is the Head, and the Church is His body (Col. 1:18, 1:24).

Christ loved the Church and gave Himself for the Church (Eph. 5:25).

The Local Church:

Is a group of believers who, according to scriptural order, regularly gather in the name and authority of Christ at a particular locale.

They gather for such things as worship, breaking bread, prayer, teaching, fellowship, etc. (Acts 2:42).

There is distinction of gender, authority, gift, and role in the local body (1 Cor. 11:2-16, 1 Cor. 14:33-34, 1 Tim. 2:11-14, Titus 1:6-13).

Often these meetings were in the homes of the believers (Rom. 16:5; Col. 4:15; 1 Cor. 16:19; Phmn. 2).

Understanding that all true believers compose the body of Christ should prompt every Christian to serve others in the Body as unto Christ Himself (Matt. 25:40). The love of Christ binds all believers together, while doctrine and location separate them into intimate gatherings for ongoing fellowship. In short, we should loathe sectarian titles which mix expressions of local and universal realities. For example: a reference to the "Plymouth

Brethren" is wrong, for "Plymouth" is local and "brethren" is universal. In the same way, the term "Roman Catholic" confuses proper terminology. To elevate and equate any group of believers with the broad term designated for the church causes undue segregation in the body – it really is nothing less than smugness to the body of Christ.

It is also common today to refer to a group of believers by referring to the building they *own*. *Chapels* and *Halls* are not people; these terms refer to the buildings in which the local assembly gathers. These terms are needful in the sense that if local churches choose to erect buildings or purchase structures the legal address must be associated with a name of some sort. Unfortunately, even the names of these structures often cause needless segregation within the body of Christ. It is noted that before the 1950's few local assemblies gathering according to New Testament principles built or owned buildings.[7] The Lord's assets were mainly designated for the Lord's work and not for temporary structures of brick and mortar. Just as Israel wanted a king to be like the surrounding nations, the New Testament church desired a building to be like Churchianity. Missionaries and full time workers over time have been significantly robbed of the Lord's portion to ensure the local church is comfortable twice a week when it gathers.

Besides the misunderstanding of proper church terminology, some gather unto things other than Christ's name. Some, like the *Baptists,* identify themselves by the doctrine of water baptism. *Lutherans* gather after the teachings of their founder, Martin Luther. *Calvinists* honour the theological framework developed by John Calvin. *Methodists* connect themselves to the early evangelistic *methods* of John and Charles Wesley. The *Presbyterians* gather to a form of church government – *presbuteros* – an elder rule. Others gather together in the name of spiritual gifts, social cliques, homeschooling, and family ties, etc. Unquestionably,

Scripture teaches the doctrine of water baptism (believer's baptism), elder rule in the local church, different evangelical methods, and the exercise and use of spiritual gifts, but we do not gather unto these; we gather in the name of Christ. Though we homeschool our children, we don't gather in the name of homeschooling. We have great commonality with the saints we gather with in the local assembly, but we don't gather to them, but for them, as unto Christ.

> Would to God that all party names and unscriptural phrases and forms which have divided the Christian world were forgot; that we might all agree to sit down together as humble, loving disciples at the feet of a common Master, to hear His word, to imbibe His Spirit, and to transcribe His life into our own.[8]
> — John Wesley

No denominations, cliques, followings, etc. should be found in the body of Christ. *Is Christ divided?* (1 Cor. 1:13). The reference to denominations is completely unbiblical. Harry A. Ironside was once asked to what denomination he belonged. He answered "I belong to the same denomination that David did" then quoted Psalm 119:63, *"I am a companion of all them that fear Thee and of them that keep Thy precepts."*[9] It is true that we will not be able to walk with (have fellowship with) all believers to the same degree, but we should have the mindset of walking as far as we can with all those who have been redeemed by the precious blood of Christ.

Fellowship is a thing of degrees based on what we hold in common, but so often believers cast others aside because of some difference in thinking, though they hold much more in common than what they disagree about. The fact of the matter is that those in the Church are not going to agree on everything on this side of glory (Eph. 4:13). Once in God's presence, we will find out that none of us had it all right – this will be one of the purest blessings of heaven. We will conclude that only God perfectly knows His own mind (Deut. 29:29).

Summary

The local assembly gathers in the name of the Lord Jesus Christ for teaching, for fellowship, for the Lord's Supper (breaking of the bread) and for prayer (Acts 2:42). The assembly is under Christ's authority, meets in His name, and gathers in His presence (Matt. 18:20) – He is Head of the Church universal and Lord of all the meetings. Terminology is important, as misapplied terms cause us to err from these infallible truths in time, the end result of which is to displace Christ with counterfeit religious façades. Misapplying scriptural terms to express a developed Church tradition or coining expressions which do not reflect the literal meaning of Scripture does not enhance our devotion to Christ, but rather stumbles us from following Him. Our allegiance is to Christ Himself; biblical reminders of Him are *second best,* and the rest will tend to pull us from the best in time.

The Blessings of the Lord's Name

In the Revelation, the Lord sent letters to seven churches in Asia Minor. Seven times He called upon five of the churches to repent of corporate sins and return to Him. To some, He warned that if they did not repent He would take away their lampstand (their church testimony would end). For two churches, Smyrna and Philadelphia, the Lord had only words of praise, no rebuke or reproof at all. Note the words of the Lord Jesus to these persecuted, but fruitful churches:

I know thy works, and where thou dwellest, even where Satan's seat is: and thou holdest fast My name, and hast not denied My faith, even in those days wherein Antipas was My faithful martyr, who was slain among you, where Satan dwelleth (Rev. 2:13).

I know thy works: behold, I have set before thee an open door, and no man can shut it: for thou hast a little strength, and hast kept My word, and hast not denied My name (Rev. 3:8)

Putting value on the name of Christ directly relates to the believer's steadfastness in faith and obedience to Scripture. The other five churches did not receive any praise from the Lord in how they were bearing up His name in the world. Believers must realize that their behaviour directly affects the honour accredited to the Lord's name. Wrong behaviour causes others to blaspheme the Lord and His name, while faithfulness and submission to Christ exalt His name.

The Lord told the churches at Smyrna and Philadelphia that He knew of their works, which were likely many, but He only highlighted their key accomplishments, and honouring His name was the overriding achievement. A. P. Gibbs composed a lovely hymn to remind believers of their calling and allegiance to Christ:

Lord Jesus, in Thy precious name, and, in that name alone;
At Thy request we gladly meet, Thy Lordship here would own.
Lord Jesus, whom, unseen, we love, as thus we muse on Thee,
We none would see, save Thee alone, thou Man of Calvary!

Let us ponder some of the privileges we have in the name of Jesus Christ and in His name alone:

To Pray in His Name

The Gospel of John, which upholds the theme of the Lord Jesus in His deity, contains several occurrences of the number *seven*. Seven is God's number of completeness and perfection and is often used in the figurative sense to convey that meaning. For example, the Lord Jesus is described as having seven horns in Revelation 5:6. In the figurative sense, a "horn" speaks of power and "seven" of perfection – the compound meaning is that the Lord Jesus is omnipotent.

John presents a strong connection between prayer and knowing and doing the will of God through "sevens." In the Gospel of John, the Lord references His Father's "will" *seven* times, His speaking only the words of His Father *seven* times, and His instruction to His disciples to pray in His name on *seven* different instances. Perfect praying centers in the will and the Word of God, it is not selfish. Of course John speaks of this in a literal fashion also:

And whatsoever ye shall ask in My name, that will I do, that the Father may be glorified in the Son. If ye shall ask any thing in My name, I will do it. If ye love Me, keep My commandments (John 14:13-15).

And this is the confidence that we have in Him, that, if we ask any thing according to His will, He heareth us (1 Jn. 5:14).

The 19th century evangelist Charles Finney summarizes what it means to pray in Christ's name:

To use this name acceptably implies a realizing sense of our character and relations, and of His character and relations; God's character and governmental position – our character and governmental position. Now, unless the mind has a realizing sense, so as really to mean what it ought to mean in using Christ's name, it does not do so acceptably. We are to use it understanding why we use it. It implies, also, the most implicit confidence in Christ's influence at His Father's court; an entire confidence that coming to God in His name we shall really obtain what we ask in His name.

When persons really and truly use the name of Christ, there is a very important sense in which they pray for Christ. I do not mean by praying for Him, that Christ needs to be prayed for as a sinner – as one who needs forgiveness, or any favour from God for Himself; but that the Church is Christ's, God having given the world to Him, in such a sense that every favour bestowed on them is regarded, governmentally, as bestowed on Him. The saints are Christ's servants. This is Christ's world in such a sense, that when the government of God grants anything to the inhabitants thereof, it yields it to Christ. Prayer has been made for Him, it is said, continually.

To pray in His name, we must ask the thing not for ourselves, because we are not our own; we do not own ourselves, and of course, therefore, we can own nothing else. The fact is, we are Christ's, and when we seek anything in Christ's name, we seek it for Him. We are Christ's servants; and as children we belong to Christ. If we want anything for ourselves, separate from Christ, to glorify ourselves, we cannot have it; but if we want it for His sake, because we belong to Him, and ask it as something to be given to us only because we belong to Him, then we can have it.[1]

Prayer is not a "name it and claim it" formula for success. Righteous praying centers in God's will and is motivated by love for the Saviour's name. When we reverently approach the throne of grace, we do so in Christ's name; let us not be guilty of praying in a way that would mock His Lordship or pervert His declared will – to do so would dishonour His name. John MacArthur puts it this way:

The waves of our indulgent, selfish, materialistic society have washed ashore on Christian theology in many forms, including the prosperity gospel. Although the Bible teaches that God is sovereign and man is His servant, the prosperity gospel implies the opposite. Teaching that claims we can demand things of God is spiritual justification for self-indulgence. It perverts prayer and takes the Lord's name in vain. It is unbiblical, ungodly, and is not directed by the Holy Spirit. Prayer begins and ends not with the needs of man but with the glory of God (John 14:13). It should be concerned primarily with who God is, what He wants, and how He can be glorified.[2]

The Lord was a man of prayer and demonstrated that prayer should precede service. Prayer demonstrates faith and dependence in the Lord to initiate, direct, and complete each matter of our lives according to His will. Besides moving the hand of God to effect His glory, prayer transforms our hearts by conforming our thinking to the mind of Christ. For those who love the name of Jesus Christ and His will, prayer is a great blessing!

To Proclaim His Name

The entire Church is to be engaged in proclaiming the gospel message of Jesus Christ *"unto the uttermost part of the earth"* (Acts 1:8). The apostles determined at the onset of their ministry to preach Christ no matter what the personal cost was to them (Acts 4:7-20). What honour it is to uphold to humankind the only name in which eternal life might be obtained. Paul taught the church at Corinth that they were the sweet aroma of Christ in the world because they represented and preached the name of Christ. May we live Christ that others might breathe in His fragrance.

> *Now thanks be unto God, which always causeth us to triumph in Christ, and maketh manifest the savour of His knowledge by us in every place. **For we are unto God a sweet savour of Christ**, in them that are saved, and in them that perish: To the one we are the savour of death unto death; and to the other the savour of life unto life. And who is sufficient for these things? For we are not as many, which corrupt the word of God: but as of sincerity, **but as of God, in the sight of God speak we in Christ*** (2 Cor. 2:14-17).

Paul was a chosen vessel to bear Christ's *"name before the Gentiles, and kings, and the children of Israel"* (Acts 9:15). What did Paul immediately do after receiving the Holy Spirit? *"He spake boldly in the name of the Lord Jesus"* (Acts 9:29). The highest occupation of the believer is to lift up the name of Jesus Christ, that Name which is above all names and the Name before which every knee shall bow.

Before the Lord Jesus ascended back to the right hand of majesty on high, He commissioned His disciples to preach the gospel. A few days after this Peter and John were venturing to

105

the temple to pray when they were solicited for alms by a man who had been lame since birth. Peter replied to the beggar: *"Silver and gold have I none, but, such as I have, give I thee. In the name of Jesus Christ of Nazareth, rise up and walk"* (Acts 3:6). Immediately, the man was helped up and began walking, leaping and praising God in the temple. Matthew Henry likens the miracle to that of salvation in Christ through new birth.

> Peter and John seem to have been led by a Divine direction, to work a miracle on a man above forty years old, who had been a cripple from his birth. Peter, in the name of Jesus of Nazareth, bade him rise up and walk. Thus, if we would attempt to good purpose the healing of men's souls, we must go forth in the name and power of Jesus Christ, calling on helpless sinners to arise and walk in the way of holiness, by faith in Him. How sweet the thought to our souls, that in respect to all the crippled faculties of our fallen nature, the name of Jesus Christ of Nazareth can make us whole! With what holy joy and rapture shall we tread the holy courts, when God the Spirit causes us to enter therein by His strength![3]

God knows that man will be the most joyful and fruitful in life by being in a right relationship with Himself. But how can they believe in Christ if they have not heard of Him (Rom. 10:14)? God has redeemed condemned pillars of dust and breathed life into us that we might proclaim His name. Sometimes, as in the case of Pharaoh, He will use the unsaved to express His greatness that the world might know Him. *"For the Scripture saith unto Pharaoh, Even for this same purpose have I raised thee up, that I might show My power in thee, and **that My name might be declared throughout all the earth*** (Rom. 9:17). God's name will be proclaimed throughout all the earth; let the believer do his or her part in this certainty. The honour of doing so will be ours throughout eternity for "this life is the dressing room for eternity!"

To Suffer for His Name

Paul was sold out to Christ and, accordingly, spoke out for Christ. "Proclaiming His name" and "suffering for His name" go hand in hand; these realities cannot be separated. *"If we suffer, we shall also reign with Him: if we deny Him, He also will deny us"* (2 Tim. 2:12). The Lord explained the connection to His disciples the night before His crucifixion. He told them that the world hated Him and would hate them also, and informed them that they would be persecuted by the world, for *"all these things will they do unto you for My name's sake"* (John 15:21).

The early church was so taken over and caught up with the person of Christ that they considered it a great privilege to suffer for His sake. In doing so, they were more able to identify with Christ. Paul passionately expressed his desire to know Christ more deeply through suffering for Him: *"That I may know Him, and the power of His resurrection, and the fellowship of his sufferings, being made conformable unto His death"* (Phil 3:10).

The apostles had been warned once already by the Pharisees not to preach Christ, but despite the threat they continued to be obedient to the Lord's commands. After being arrested a second time, we read that the Sanhedrin had them beaten and then commanded them not speak in the name of Jesus Christ before letting them go. What did they do? *"And they departed from the presence of the council, rejoicing that they were counted worthy to suffer shame for His name. And daily in the temple, and in every house, they ceased not to teach and preach Jesus Christ"* (Acts 5:41-42). They had settled the death question and determined that preaching Christ was more honourable than living without declaring His name.

The assurance of God's Word gave the apostles hope for the future and an infusion of joy while bearing tremendous pain and suffering. Consequently, the Lord's disciples faced death with the same hope and joy that their Saviour did. History records that Aegeas crucified Andrew, Peter's brother, for his faith in Christ. Seeing his cross before him, Andrew bravely spoke, "O cross, most welcome and longed for! With a willing mind, joyfully and desirously, I come to thee, being the scholar of Him which did hang on thee: because I have always been thy lover, and have coveted to embrace thee."[4] How could Andrew approach his cross with anticipation and joy? He had watched the Lord approach His cross in the same manner.

During the deepest trials of life, hundreds of thousands of believers, throughout the Church Age, have found it is possible to have present joy in God's future promises, even while enduring torture and staring death in the face. They did so in the name of Jesus Christ. During the reign of Queen Mary, thousands of Christians were burned at the stake in England for their testimony of Christ. On July 15, 1556 was one such occasion when Julius Palmer, Thomas Askin, and John Guin, having been sentenced to death by burning, had a triumphant entrance into our gracious Lord's presence.

Askin and one John Guin had been sentenced the day before, and Mr. Palmer, on the fifteenth, was brought up for final judgement. Execution was ordered to follow the sentence, and at five o'clock in the same afternoon, at a place called the Sand-pits, these three martyrs were fastened to a stake. After devoutly praying together, they sung the Thirty-first Psalm.

When the fire was kindled, and it had seized their bodies, without an appearance of enduring pain, they continued to cry, "Lord Jesus, strengthen us! Lord Jesus receive our souls!" until animation was suspended and human suffering was past. It

108

is remarkable, that, when their heads had fallen together in a mass as it were by the force of the flames, and the spectators thought Palmer as lifeless, his tongue and lips again moved, and were heard to pronounce the name of Jesus, to whom be glory and honour forever![5]

If ye be reproached for the name of Christ, happy are ye; for the spirit of glory and of God resteth upon you: on their part He is evil spoken of, but on your part He is glorified (1 Pet. 4:14).

If we suffer, we shall also reign with Him; if we deny Him, He also will deny us (2 Tim. 2:12).

To Gather in His Name

Paul speaks of the entire body of Christ, that is all true believers, as the House of God – His living temple on earth (1 Tim. 3:15; 1 Pet. 2:5). In 1 Corinthians 6:19-20, he exhorts individual believers to understand that their bodies are temples of the Holy Spirit and that they should render their whole self for the glory of God. Paul also refers to the local assembly as the temple of God (1 Cor. 3:16-17). The local assembly of believers is a lampstand (Rev. 2:5), a testimony of God's grace which outshines God's glory to a lost world, while lifting praise heavenward to refresh the heart of God. The extent that each local church realizes this end will depend on their devotion to the name of Christ. C. H. Mackintosh writes:

> The power in an assembly will very much depend upon the measure in which each member thereof is gathered in integrity of heart to the name of Jesus. If I am gathered to a party holding peculiar opinions – if I am attracted by the people, or by the teaching – if, in a word, it be not the power of the Holy Ghost, leading me to the true Centre of God's assembly, I shall only prove a hindrance, a weight, a cause of weakness, I

shall be to an assembly what a waster is to a candle; and instead of adding to the general light and usefulness, I shall do the very reverse.[6]

Although the local church gathers together for different reasons (Acts 2:42), all of the meetings possess a central theme – we gather in the name of the Lord Jesus and, hence, in the authority of that Name. Paul ensured that the church at Corinth understood this fact, *"In the name of our Lord Jesus Christ, when ye are gathered together"* (1 Cor. 5:4). Whether it is about a simple feast of bread and wine to remember Him and publicly proclaim the value of His death, or around His Word to learn His mind, or round His mercy seat to tell Him our needs or to encourage His people in pressing forward to their high-calling in Christ – we meet with Him and in His name. The Lord and His presence alone draws us to every church meeting. I want to be at every meeting because the Lord will be at every meeting. When a believer justifies careless absenteeism, in effect he or she is casting a vote to close down the assembly and remove Christ's name from the community! On the subject of gathering in Christ's name, C. H. Mackintosh writes:

> Of the many favors conferred upon us by our ever-gracious Lord, one of the very highest is the privilege of being present in the assembly of His beloved people, where He has recorded His name. We may assert with all possible confidence that every true lover of Christ will delight to be found where He has promised to be. We may rest assured that any one who willfully neglects the assembly is in a cold, dead, dangerous state of soul. To neglect the assembling of ourselves is to take the first step on the inclined plane that leads down to the total abandonment of Christ and His precious interests.[7]

The Lord extended this promise to His disciples, *"For where two or three are gathered together in My name, there am I in the midst of them"* (Matt. 18:19-20). The Lord told the thief on the cross, *"Today you will be with Me in paradise"* (Luke 23:43, NKJV). Paradise is wherever the Lord is, meaning that the closest experience of heaven itself on this side of glory is to be gathered together with other believers in the presence of the Lord Jesus. The gathering of the local assembly should be loved for it is a visible reminder to the world that Christ has a record of Himself there – a testimony (a lampstand) in the world.

The purpose of our church meetings is not to gather to gifted men, ministries, schooling preferences, occupational ranks, ethnic orientations, civil status or organizing causes. We gather to be with the Lord, to worship Him, to honour Him, to ask Him for help in learning His mind and to refresh and encourage His people. What would be the effect if the local church gathered in full privilege to the name of Jesus Christ and His name alone?

It would be the very atmosphere of Heaven itself; the name of Jesus would be as ointment poured forth; every eye would be fixed on Him, every heart absorbed with Him, and there would be a more powerful testimony to His name and presence in our midst than could be rendered by the most brilliant gift.[8]

— C. H. M.

To Praise His Name

But let all those that put their trust in Thee rejoice: let them ever shout for joy, because Thou defendest them: let them also that love Thy name be joyful in Thee (Ps. 5:11).

Serve the Lord with gladness: come before His presence with singing (Ps. 100:2).

Praise ye the Lord. Praise, O ye servants of the Lord, praise the name of the Lord. Blessed be the name of the Lord from this time forth and for evermore. From the rising of the sun unto the going down of the same the Lord's name is to be praised. The Lord is high above all nations, and His glory above the heavens. Who is like unto the Lord our God, who dwelleth on high? (Ps. 113:1-5).

Singing is a natural means of praising the Lord for His goodness and protection. More than seventy-four references to the Lord's people singing appear in the book of Psalms. What are they singing about? The Lord's name (Jehovah) is mentioned 645 times in the Psalms – the righteous love to sing of His name. To the believer, the Lord's name refers to His character and attributes. His presence provides joy in life now, and His promises yield hope for the future.

The Psalmist declares, *"O Lord, our Lord, how excellent is thy name in all the earth, who hast set Thy glory above the heavens!"* (Ps. 8:1). Commenting to this exaltation in praise Adam Clarke writes:

How excellent is thy name in all the earth!—How illustrious is the name of Jesus throughout the world! His incarnation, birth, humble and obscure life, preaching, miracles, passion, death, resurrection, and ascension, are celebrated through the whole world. His religion, the gifts and graces of His Spirit, His people—Christians—His Gospel and the preachers of it are everywhere spoken of. No name is so universal, no power and influence so generally felt, as those of the Saviour of mankind. Amen.[9]

To Honour His Name

Paul exhorts the Christians at Colosse to consider every aspect of their conduct and speech as an approval or disapproval of the name of Jesus Christ. *"And whatsoever ye do in word or deed, do all in the name of the Lord Jesus, giving thanks to God and the Father by Him"* (Col. 3:17). Each believer functions as an ambassador of Christ on earth (2 Cor. 5:20); we are to represent the Lord and conduct His affairs on earth in a manner which would honour Him. We are Christians, *Christ-ones*. Warren Wiersbe summarizes what it means to bear up the name of the Lord Jesus as a Christian.

As Christians, we bear the name of Christ. The word *Christian* is found only three times in the entire New Testament (Acts 11:26; 26:28; 1 Peter 4:16). The name was given originally as a term of contempt, but gradually it became a name of honour. The name of Christ, then, means *identification:* we belong to Jesus Christ. But His name also means *authority*. A man's name signed to a check authorizes the withdrawal of money from the bank. The President's name signed to a bill makes it a law. In the same way, it is in the name of Jesus Christ that we have the authority to pray (John 14:13-14; 16:23-26). Because Jesus Christ is God, and He has died for us, we have authority in His name.

All that we say and do should be associated with the name of Jesus Christ. By our words and our works, we should glorify His name. If we permit anything into our lives that cannot be associated with the name of Jesus, then we are sinning. We must do and say everything on the authority of His name and for the honour of His name. Bearing the name of Jesus is a great privilege, but it is also a tremendous responsibility.[10]

As we ponder the great honour of being intimately associated with the name of Jesus Christ, we do well to consider Paul's

113

remarks to the church at Thessalonica (a church under intense persecution): *"That the name of our Lord Jesus Christ may be glorified in you, and ye in Him, according to the grace of our God and the Lord Jesus Christ. Now we beseech you, brethren, by the coming of our Lord Jesus Christ, and by our gathering together unto Him..."* (2 Thess. 1:12-2:1). Though all mankind can witness the glory of God, only the Spirit-filled believer experiences the glory of God now through the name of Jesus Christ. Those who know His glory now will be glorified with Him soon, for He is coming back to gather together all true believers unto Himself. Then we will ever be with the Lord (1 Thess. 4:17)!

The opposite of blaspheming God is to honour Him. How do we honour God? By exercising faith in His revealed will, as declared in Scripture, which results in rendering to God the reverence and service due His holy name. Hallowed be Thy Name!

"I Will Sanctify My Great Name"

The night prior to His crucifixion, the Lord Jesus uttered a prayer which genuinely and purely declared the reason for His sojourn on earth. The Lord intimately conversed with His Father, *"I have manifested Thy name"* (John 17:6). What does it mean to manifest God's name? Attributes of *name* and *person* are inseparable; the Lord Jesus, in living flesh, had put God on display. God entered the realm of space and time in human form to declare His moral excellence, the power of His greatness, and rich essence of His life. Consequently, man has been summonsed to appreciate the goodness of God and thankfully some have responded to drawing effect of God's love and have received and experienced eternal life in Christ.

> *That which was from the beginning, which we have heard, which we have seen with our eyes, which we have looked upon, and our hands have handled, of the Word of life; (For the life was manifested, and we have seen it, and bear witness, and show unto you that eternal life, which was with the Father, and was manifested unto us.)* (1 John 1:1-2).

All those who knew the Lord Jesus witnessed in His life the declaration of "Hallowed be Thy name." The believer must follow Christ's example (1 Pet. 2:21); to exhale in one breath "Hallowed be Thy name," and inhale human traditions, secular philosophies, and the rudiments of the world in the next is pure hypocrisy and dishonouring to God's name. On this point, Thomas Brooks wrote: "In divine account a man knows no more than he doth. Profession without practice will but make a man twicefold a child of darkness."[1]

The prophet Ezekiel was used as God's mouthpiece to declare a powerful message to the nation of Israel. In it, God's people learned of His anger concerning their ungodly behaviour. Their insolence and idolatry had done nothing less than caused the Lord's name to be blasphemed among the nations:

> *When they came to the nations, wherever they went, they profaned My holy name -- when they said of them, 'These are the people of the Lord, and yet they have gone out of His land.' But I had concern for My holy name, which the house of Israel had profaned among the nations wherever they went. "Therefore say to the house of Israel, 'Thus says the Lord God: "I do not do this for your sake, O house of Israel, but **for My holy name's sake**, which you have profaned among the nations wherever you went. And **I will sanctify My great name**, which has been profaned among the nations, which you have profaned in their midst; and the nations shall know that I am the Lord," says the Lord God, "when I am hallowed in you before their eyes* (Ezek. 36:20-23, NKJV).

It is indeed a sad commentary when God's people fall so deeply that they profane the Lord's name among the nations. When the heathen exclaim, "These people are so repulsive that their God must be even worse," a terrible blasphemy of God's good name has occurred – yet this is exactly what many Moslems, Hindus, and Buddhists say of Christianity and of Christ today. The conduct of the professing church, in general, is putrid. Yet, God's name will be sanctified one way or another – He will do it by Himself, even if we choose not to!

How will God's name be sanctified and hallowed through the nation of Israel? In a future day, God will create in them a new heart and will pour out His Spirit upon them: *"A new heart also will I give you, and a new Spirit will I put within you"* (Ezek. 36:26).

If our heart beats for Christ and we are attentive to the guidance of the Holy Spirit, we will quickly recognize anything that disdains the name of the Lord and be prompted to respond in the power of the Spirit. So how will you sanctify God's Name? Determine now what you will do in different situations so that you will be ready to properly respond when God's name is dishonoured. Here are six suggestions:

1. **Bestow honour when speaking of the Lord Jesus.** The Epistles set forth an example for all believers to follow. In penning Scripture, the apostles were careful to connect the name of "Jesus" with a proper title of exaltation or in an arrangement that demonstrated His personal equality with God the Father or the Holy Spirit. If you utter that sweet name which above all names, "Jesus," be sure in the same breath to acknowledge His lofty station – He is Lord of all. The Lord Jesus Christ has an acquired position above all that is created; let us not refer to Him as a mere man who once trod terrestrial courses in time. By acknowledging Him as Lord and Christ you are proclaiming to the world the essence of the gospel message and that you have trusted it. *"I will declare Thy name unto my brethren: in the midst of the congregation will I praise Thee."* (Ps. 22:22).

2. **Beware of unnatural unions.** Realize that everyone who names the name of Christ and calls Him Lord is not a believer (Matt. 7:21). Presently, 98 million individuals claim

to be "born again" in the United States.[2] Does the moral character of our society indicate that one in three are Spirit indwelt temples of God? We clearly live in days of spiritual deception and complacency. It is a trick of the enemy to identify with the name of the Lord in order to forge some unnatural relationship so that the work of God might be brought to naught. In Genesis 30:27, Laban used the name of the Lord in a familiar sense to camouflage the evil contract he was presenting to Jacob concerning wages. This ploy was also used by the enemy on both Zerubbabel and Nehemiah in an attempt to stop the work of rebuilding the temple and the wall about Jerusalem, respectively. Unfortunately, this tactic ensnared Jehoshaphat into ratifying an aberrant covenant with wicked King Ahab. Judge the fruit of others, dear believer (Matt. 12:33-34); don't be conned by someone who names the name of Christ but blasphemes the Lord's name by their conduct.

3. **Respond when the Lord's name is used vainly.** How will you respond when you hear someone use the Lord's name in vain? As a rule of thumb, do you think it is better just to ignore the slander or to admonish the person? The latter is the right response, though your response should consider whether the person claims to be a Christian or not. A professing Christian should receive an immediate and forthright rebuke. For the unsaved individual, may I suggest connecting his or her response to the third of the Ten Commandments: *"Thou shalt not take the name of the Lord thy God in vain; for the Lord will not hold him guiltless that taketh His name in vain"* (Ex. 20:7). By scripturally demonstrating to the unsaved person that they have violated God's law and stand guilty before their Creator and Judge, the gospel message of Jesus Christ will really

seem like good news. The situation lends itself to a great evangelical opportunity. *"But sanctify the Lord God in your hearts: and be ready always to give an answer to every man that asketh you a reason of the hope that is in you **with meekness and fear**"* (1 Pet. 3:15). If in a group of people, you may be able to address the matter in a pointed, but non-brutal, method by saying something like, "Excuse me, were you just praying right then, or were you taking the Lord's name in vain?" The point is made without any further discussion.

4. **Develop sensitivity to unscriptural terminology and unbiblical religious terms.** In time, unscriptural terminology and religious terms tend to corrupt holiness and produce unscriptural Church practices. We are more likely to accept false doctrine through the medium of music than preaching, so be alert. Scan the chorus books and hymnal, and purge the songs which contain phrases propagating false doctrines, contextual errors, or self-exaltation. J. N. Darby once said "that the devil was never more satanic than when he has a Bible in his hands." Understanding that the adversary seeks to pervert the meaning of Scripture and the meanings of words ought to provoke every believer to be more diligent in the Word of God. Scripture is infallible, true and eternal; it is our defense against being led astray or drifting in our terminology which eventually leads to erroneous Church traditions and practices.

5. **Remove man-devised offices, titles, and unbiblical traditions from your church gatherings.** Hopefully those in church leadership will uphold the holiness of God's name also and see the value of removing that which tarnishes God's name and draws the believer's focus away from the

Lord. Several years ago, a man visiting our church meeting asked why we were not covering the emblems with a
white linen cloth after each had been passed during the
Lord's Supper. I asked him why he thought it should be
done. He responded, "It shows that the matter is finished."
My next question irritated him a bit, "Is that a scriptural
practice?" He said, "No, I guess not, but that is what we
did in the church I came from." "In other words, you
would like us to initiate the same unbiblical tradition
here?" There was no more discussion; the point was made.
It is perhaps permissible to cover the emblems, but to state
that one must is wrong. Over time, such things become
rigid, and most people don't even know why things are the
way they are. Scripture will provide the best answer, and
simplicity will guide where Scripture is silent (2 Cor.
11:3).

6. **Practice Holiness.** The command proceeds from the Lord
   Himself to His people: *"Be ye holy for I am holy"* (1 Pet.
   1:16). Paul explains what it means to practice holiness:

   > *Prove all things; hold fast that which is good. Abstain
   > from all appearance of evil. And the very God of peace
   > sanctify you wholly...* (1 Thess. 5:21-23).

May each believer pursue the example of the Lord Jesus,
who in all things, whether in word or in deed, declared the holiness of His Father in an honourable way. There are degrees of
wisdom, degrees of understanding, degrees of gift and abilities,
but there are no degrees of purity or holiness; thus, the believer
is to *"put difference between Holy and Unholy"* (Lev. 10:10).
God is perfectly holy, and He instructs His children to be no less
holy in conduct: *"Be ye holy, for I am holy."* This is a great calling and, as Leonard Ravenhill correctly surmises, a miraculous

feat: "The greatest miracle that God can do today is to take an unholy man out of an unholy world, and make that man holy and put him back into that unholy world and keep him holy in it."[3]

The last chapter of the Bible foretells a marvelous and eternal truth concerning the name of Christ: *"And there shall be no more curse: but the throne of God and of the Lamb shall be in it; and His servants shall serve Him: And they shall see His face; and His name shall be in their foreheads"* (Rev. 22:3-4). Long after the expanse of time has been exhausted, every believer will be shining forth the glorious name of the Lord. With the Saviour's face before us and His name universally declared by all the redeemed, can there be any question to the brilliant hues of heaven – the splendor of the Lord shall be witnessed everywhere. May we all yield now to our eternal destiny in Christ – to worship the Lord and honour His great name! Hallowed be Thy name forever and ever.

Appendix A
Names and Titles of Christ

Over 400 names and titles of Christ found in Scripture are listed below. Why not study and contemplate a particular name of the Lord Jesus Christ each day of the year. To this end, the reader may find the following devotional resources helpful:

Names of God by Nathan Stone
Names of Christ by T. C. Horton and Charles Hurlburt
Names of the Holy Spirit by Ray Pritchard

As you behold the glory of the Lord, may you be changed into the same image from glory to glory, by the Spirit of the Lord (2 Cor. 3:18).

~ A ~

Advocate: (1 Jn. 2:1)
Alien unto My Mother's Children: (Ps. 69:9)
All and in All: (Col. 3:11)
Almighty: (Rev. 1:8)
Altogether Lovely One: (Song. 5:16)
Alpha: (Rev. 1:8)
Altar: (Heb. 13:10)

Amen: (Rev. 3:14)
Anchor: (Heb. 6:19)
Ancient of Days: (Dan. 7:9-11; Rev. 1:13-16)
Angel (or Messenger): (Gen. 48:16; Ex. 23:20-21)
Angel of His presence: (Isa. 63:9)
Angel (Redeeming): (Gen 48:16)
Angel (of the Lord): (Ex. 3:2, Judg. 2:1-1)
Anointed: (Ps. 2:2)
Apostle: (Heb. 3:1)
Arm of the Lord: (Isa. 51:9-10, 53:1)
Atoning Sacrifice: (1 Jn. 2:2)
Author of Our Faith: (Heb. 12:2)
Author of Life: (Acts 3:15)
Author of Salvation: (Hebrews 2:10)

~B~

Babe: (Lk. 2:16)
Balm of Gilead: (Jer. 8:22)
Beginning (the): (Col. 1:18, Rev. 22:13)
Beginning of the Creation of God: (Rev. 3:14)
Begotten of Father: (John 1:14)
Beloved: (Matt. 12:18, Eph. 1:6)
Beloved Son (God's): (Matt. 17:5)
Bishop (of souls): (1 Pet. 2:25)
Blessed and Only Potentate: (1 Tim. 6:15)
Blessed Hope: (Titus 2:13)
Branch (the righteous): (Jer. 23:5)
Branch of the Lord: (Isa. 4:2)
Branch (out of Jesse - David): (Isa. 11:1)
Branch (My Servant): (Zech. 3:8)
Branch (the Man): (Zech. 6:12)
Bread of Life: (John 6:8)

Bridegroom: (Matt. 9:15)
Bright and Morning Star: (Rev. 22:16)
Brightness of the Father's glory: (Heb. 1:3)
Bronze Serpent on the Pole: (John 3:14)

~C~

Captain of the Lord's Host: (Josh. 5:14)
Captain of Salvation: (Heb. 2:10)
Carpenter: (Mark 6:3)
Carpenter's Son: (Matt. 13:55)
Chief Shepherd: (1 Pet. 5:4)
Chief Cornerstone: (1 Pet. 2:6)
Chiefest Among Ten Thousand: (Song. 5:10)
Child: (Isa. 7:16; 9:6)
Child Jesus (the): (Luke 2:27; 2:43)
Chosen of God: (1 Pet. 2:4; Luke 23:35)
Chosen One: (Isa. 42:1)
Christ: (Matt. 1:16; Luke 9:20)
Christ (the Christ – Messiah): (Matt. 16:20; Mark 14:61)
Christ, a King: (Luke 23:2)
Christ Jesus: (Acts 19:4: Rom. 3:24)
Christ Jesus our Lord: (1 Tim. 1:12; Rom. 8:39)
Christ of God: (Luke 9:20)
Christ our Life: (Col. 3:4)
Christ, the Chosen of God: (Luke 23:35)
Christ the Lord: (Luke 2:11)
Christ, the power of God: (1 Cor. 1:24)
Christ the wisdom of God: (1 Cor. 1:24)
Christ, the Son of God: (Acts 9:20)
Christ, Son of the Blessed: (Mark 14:61)
Comforter: (Isa. 61:2; Jn. 14:16)

Commander: (Isa. 55:4)
Consolation of Israel: (Luke 2:25)
Corn of Wheat: (Jn. 12:24)
Cornerstone: (Eph. 2:20)
Counselor: (Isa. 9:6)
Covenant of the People: (Isa. 42:6)
Covert: (Isa. 32:2)
Creator: (John 1:3; Col. 1:16; Heb. 1:2)
Crown of Glory: (Isa. 28:5)

~D~

David: (Jer. 30:9)
Day Star: (2 Pet. 1:19)
Daysman: (Job 9:33)
Dayspring: (Luke 1:78)
Dear Son (God's): Col. 1:13
Deliverer: (Rom. 11:26)
Desire of All Nations: (Hag. 2:7)
Diadem of Beauty: (Isa. 28:5)
The Door: (John 10:7)

~E~

Elect: (Isaiah 42:1)
Elect of God: (Isa. 42:1)
Emmanuel (Immanuel): (Isa. 7:14)
End (of the creation of God): (Rev. 3:14; 22:13)
Ensign: (Isa. 11:10)
Eternal Life: (1 Jn. 5:20)
Everlasting Father: (Isa. 9:6)
Everlasting God: (Isa. 40:28)

Everlasting Light: (Isa. 60:20)
Everlasting Strength (Isa. 26:4)
Express Image of God (of His person): (Heb. 1:3)

~F~

Faithful and True: (Rev. 19:11)
Faithful Witness: (Rev. 1:5)
Faithful and True Witness: (Rev. 3:14)
Finisher of Our Faith: (Heb. 12:2)
First: (Rev. 1:17; 2:8; 22:13)
First Begotten: (Heb. 1:6)
First Begotten of the Dead: (Rev. 1:5)
Firstborn (God's): (Ps. 89:27)
Firstborn Among Many Brethren: (Rom. 8:29)
Firstborn from the Dead: (Col. 1:18)
Firstborn of All Creation: (Col. 1:15)
First Fruits: (Ex. 22:29)
First Fruits of Them that Slept (died): (1 Cor. 15:20)
Foundation: (Isa. 28:16)
Fountain: (Zech. 13:1)
Forerunner: (Heb. 6:20)
Friend of sinners: (Matt. 11:19)

~G~

Gate: (John 10:7)
Gift of God: (John 4:10)
Glorious Lord Jesus Christ: (Jas. 2:1)
Glorious Throne: (Isa. 22:23)
Glory of God: (Isa. 60:1)

Glory of Israel: (Luke 2:32)
God (deity): (John 1:1; Rom. 9:5; 1 Tim. 3:16)
God Blessed Forever: (Rom. 9:5)
God Manifest in Flesh: (1 Tim. 3:16)
God of Israel, the Saviour: (Isa. 45:15)
God of the Whole Earth: (Isa. 54:5)
God of All the Earth: (Isa. 54:5)
God Our Saviour: (1 Tim. 2:3)
God and Saviour of Israel: (Isa. 45:15)
God over All: (Rom. 9:5)
God's Dear Son: (Col. 1:13)
God the One and Only: (John 1:18)
God With Us: (Matt. 1:23)
Good Shepherd: (John 10:11, 14)
Good Teacher: (Mark 10:17)
Good Master: (Matt. 19:16)
Governor: (Matt. 2:6)
Great God and Saviour: (Titus 2:13)
Great High Priest: (Heb. 4:14)
Great Light: (Isa. 9:2)
Great Prophet: (Luke 7:16)
Great Shepherd of the Sheep: (Heb.13:20)
Guarantee (surety): (Heb. 7:22)
Guide: (Ps. 48:14)

~H~

He that Filleth All in All: (Eph. 1:23)
He that Liveth: (Rev. 1:18)
He that Shall Come: (Heb. 10:36-37)
Head of Every Man: (1 Cor. 11:3)

Head of the Church (body): (Eph. 1:22-23; 5:23)
Head of the Corner: (Matt. 21:42)
Heir of All Things: (Heb. 1:2)
Helper (my): (Heb. 13:6)
Hidden Manna (the): (Rev. 2:17)
Hiding Place: (Isa. 32:2)
High Priest: (Heb. 4:14)
High Tower (my): (Ps. 18:2)
Higher than the Heavens: (Heb. 7:26)
Holiness: (1 Cor.1:30)
Holy Child Jesus: (Acts 4:30)
Holy One: (Ps. 16:10; Acts 3:14)
Holy One of God: (Mark 1:24)
Holy One of Israel: (Isa. 41:14; 54:5)
Holy and Righteous One: (Acts 3:14)
Holy servant Jesus: (Acts 4:30)
Holy thing: (Luke 1:35)
Hope (our): (1 Tim. 1:1)
Hope of Israel: (Jer. 17:3)
Horn of salvation: (Luke 1:69)

~I~

I AM: (John 8:58)
    I am the Bread of Life (John 6:35).
    I am the Light of the World (John 9:5).
    I am the Good Shepherd (John 10:11).
    I am the Door (John 10:9).
    I am the Resurrection (John 11:25).
    I am the true Vine (John 15:1).
    I am the Way, the Truth and the Life (John 14:6).
Image of God: (2 Cor. 4:4)
Image of the Invisible God: (Col. 1:15)

Immanuel: (Isa. 7:14; Matt. 1:23)
Incarnate: (John 1:14)
Indescribable gift: (2 Cor. 9:15)
Innocent man (Matt. 27:19)
Intercessor: (Heb. 7:25)
Israel: (Isa. 49:3)

~J~

Jehovah (Yahweh): (Isa. 26:4; 40:3)
Jehovah's (Yahweh's) fellow: (Zech. 13:7)
Jesus: (Matt. 1:21)
Jesus Christ: (Matt. 1:1; John 1:17)
Jesus Christ our Lord: (Rom. 1:3)
Jesus Christ our Saviour: (Titus 3:6)
Jesus Christ the Righteous: (1 Jn. 2:1)
Jesus of Nazareth: (Mark 1:24; Luke 24:19)
Jesus of Nazareth, King of the Jews: (John 19:19)
Jesus, the King of the Jews: (Matt. 27:37)
Jesus, the Son of God: (Heb. 4:14)
Jesus, the Son of Joseph: (John 6:42)
Judge: (Acts 10:42; 2 Tim. 4:1)
Just Man: (Matt. 27:19)
Just One: (Acts 3:14; Acts 7:52)
Just Person: (Matt. 27:24)

~K~

King: (Matt. 21:5)
King of glory (Ps. 24:7-10)
King of the ages (Rev. 15:3)

King of Israel: (John 1:49)
King of the Jews: (Matt. 2:2)
King of Saints: (Rev. 15:3)
King of Kings: (1 Tim. 6:15; Rev. 17:14)
King of Glory: (Ps. 24:7-10)
King of Zion: (Matt. 21:5)
King over all the earth: (Zech. 14:9)
Kinsman (Ruth 2:14)

~L~

Ladder (Jacob's): (Gen. 28:12, Jn. 1:51)
Lamb: (Rev. 5:6, 8)
Lamb of God: (John 1:29)
Last: (Rev. 1:17; 2:8; 22:13)
The Last Adam: (1 Cor. 15:45)
The Laver: (Ex. 30:18; Zech. 13:1; Eph 5:26)
Lawgiver: (Isa. 33:22)
Leader: (Isa. 55:4)
Life: (John 14:6)
Lifter up of Mine Head (the): (Ps. 3:3)
Light: (John 8:12)
Light, Everlasting: (Isa. 60:20)
Light of Israel: (Isa. 10:17)
Light of Men: (John 1:4)
Light of the City: (Rev. 21:23)
Light of the World: (John 8:12)
Light to the Gentiles: (Isa. 42:6)
Light (true): (John 1:9)
Lion of the Tribe of Judah: (Rev. 5:5)
Living Bread: (John 6:51)
Living Stone: (1 Pet. 2:4)
Lord: (Rom. 1:3)

Lord Almighty: (Jas. 5:4)
Lord and My God: (John 20:28)
Lord and Saviour Jesus Christ: (2 Pet. 1:11; 3:18)
Lord Christ: (Col. 3:24)
Lord from Heaven: (1 Cor. 15:47)
Lord God Almighty: (Rev. 15:3)
Lord God Omnipotent: (Rev. 19:6)
Lord Jesus: (Acts 7:59; Col. 3:17; 1 Thess. 4:2)
Lord Jesus Christ: (Acts 11:17; 16:31)
Lord Jesus Christ our Saviour: (Titus 1:4)
Lord, Mighty in Battle: (Psalm 24:8)
Lord of All: (Acts 10:36)
Lord of Lords: (Rev. 17:14; 19:16)
Lord of Hosts: (Isaiah 44:6)
Lord of the Dead and Living: (Rom. 14:9)
Lord of the Sabbath: (Mark 2:28)
Lord Our Righteousness: (Jer. 23:6)
Lord of Glory: (Jas. 2:1)
Lord Over All: (Rom. 10:12)
Lord, Strong and Mighty: (Ps. 24:8)
Lord, the, Our Righteousness: (Jer. 23:6)
Lord, Your Holy One: (Isa. 43:15)
Lord, Your Redeemer: (Isa. 43:14)
Lord's Christ: (Luke 2:26)

~M~

Maker (thy): (Isa. 54:5)
Man (the): (John 19:5)
Man Approved of God: (Acts 2:22)
Man Christ Jesus: (1 Tim. 2:5)
Man of Sorrows: (Isa. 53:3)
Man Who is Close to Me (the Lord): (Zech. 13:7)

Manna: (Ex. 16:11; John 6:32; Rev. 2:17)
Master: (Matt 23:8, John 13:13)
Mediator (the only): (1 Tim. 2:5)
Mediator of a Better Covenant: (Heb. 8:6)
Mediator of the New Covenant: (Heb. 12:24)
Merciful High Priest: (Heb. 2:17)
Mercy Seat: (Rom. 3:24-25)
Messenger of the Covenant: (Mal. 3:1)
Messiah: (John 1:41)
Messiah the Prince: (Dan. 9:25)
Mighty God: (Isa. 9:6)
Mighty One of Israel: (Isa. 30:29)
Mighty One of Jacob: (Isa. 49:26)
Mighty to Save: (Isa. 63:1)
Minister of the Circumcision: (Rom. 15:8)
Minister of the Sanctuary: (Heb. 8:2)
Morning Star: (Rev. 22:16)
Most Holy: (Dan. 9:24)
Most Mighty: (Ps. 45:3)

~N~

Nail in a Sure Place (a): (Isa. 22:22-25)
Nazarene: (Matt. 2:23)
Nobleman: (Luke 19:12)

~O~

Offering: (Eph. 5:2; Heb. 10:10)
Offspring of David: (Rev. 22:16)
Ointment Poured Forth (Song. 1:3)
One and Only (the): (John 1:14)
One and Only Son: (John 3:16, 18)

Omega: (Rev. 1:8)
Only Begotten: (John 1:14; 3:16)
Only Wise God, Our Saviour: (Jude 1:25)
Overcomer (the): (John 16:33)
Overseer (Bishop): (1 Pet. 2:25)
Own Son (God's): (Rom. 8:32)

~P~

Passover (our): (1 Cor. 5:7)
Peace (our): (Eph. 2:14)
Physician: (Matt. 9:12; Luke 4:23)
Plant of Renown (a): (Ezek. 34:29)
Polished Shaft (a): (Isa. 49:2)
Portion of Jacob (the): (Jer. 10:16)
Potentate: (1 Tim. 6:15)
Potter (our): (Isa. 64:8)
Power of God: (1 Cor. 1:24)
Physician: (Matt. 9:12)
Precious Cornerstone: (Isa. 28:16)
Priest: (Heb. 7:17)
Priest Forever: (Heb. 5:6)
Prince and a Saviour: (Acts 5:31)
Prince of Life: (Acts 3:15)
Prince of Peace: (Isa. 9:6)
Prince of Princes (the): Dan. 8:25)
Prince of the Kings of the Earth: (Rev. 1:5)
Prophet: (Deut. 18:15, 18; Matt. 21:11)
Prophet Mighty in Deed and Word: (Luke 24:19)
Prophet of the Hightest (the): (Luke 1:76)
Propitiation: (1 Jn. 2:2)
Power of God: (1 Cor. 1:24)
Purifier: (Mal 3:3)

~Q~

Quickening (Life-Giving) Spirit: (1 Cor. 15:45)

~R~

Rabbi: (John 1:49; 3:2)
Rabboni: (John 20:16)
Radiance of God's glory: (Heb. 1:3)
Ransom: (1 Tim. 2:6)
Reaper: (Rev. 14:15)
Redeemer: (Isa. 59:20)
Redemption: (1 Cor. 1:30)
Refiner: (Mal. 3:3)
Refuge: (Num. 35:6; Isa. 25:4; Heb. 6:18)
Resting Place: (Jer. 50:6)
Restorer: (Ps. 23:2)
Resurrection and the Life (the): (John 11:25)
Rewarder (a): (Heb. 11:6)
Redemption: (1 Cor. 1:30)
Righteous Branch: (Jer. 23:5)
Righteous Judge: (2 Tim. 4:8)
Righteous One: (Acts 7:52; 22:14)
Righteous Servant: (Isa. 53:11)
Righteousness: (Jer. 23:6; 33:16; 1 Cor. 1:30)
Rising Sun: (Luke 1:78)
River of Water in a Dry Place: (Isa. 32:2)
Rock: (1 Cor. 10:4)
Rock of My Strength: (Ps. 62:7)
Rock of Offence: (1 Pet. 2:8)
Rod: (Isa. 11:1)

Root of David: (Rev. 5:5; 22:16)
Root of Jesse: (Isa. 11:10)
Rose of Sharon: (Song. 2:1)
Ruler in Israel: (Micah 5:2)
Ruler of Creation: (Rev. 3:14)
Ruler of the Kings of the Earth: (Rev. 1:5)

~S~

Sacrifice: (1 Jn. 2:2)
Sacrifice to God: (Luke 2:30)
Salvation of God: (Luke 2:30)
Sanctification: (1 Cor. 1:30)
Sanctuary: (Isa. 8:14)
Saviour: (Luke 2:11)
Saviour, Jesus Christ: (2 Tim. 1:10; Titus 2:13)
Saviour of the Body (Church): (Eph. 5:23)
Saviour of the World: (1 Jn. 4:14)
Scapegoat: (Lev. 16:20, Isa. 53:6)
Scepter: (Num. 24:17)
Second Man (the): (1 Cor. 15:47)
Seed of Abraham: (Gal. 3:16, 19)
Seed of David: (2 Tim. 2:8)
Seed of the Woman: (Gen. 3:15)
Sent of the Father: (John 17:18)
Servant: (Isa. 42:1; 53:11)
Servant of rulers: (Isa. 49:7)
Shadow from the Heat (a): (Isa. 25:4)
Shadow of a Great Rock: (Isa. 32:2)
Shepherd: (Mark 14:27)
Shepherd and Overseer of souls: (1 Pet. 2:25)
Shepherd of Israel: (Ps. 80:1)
Shield (my): (Ps. 3:3)

Shiloh: (Gen. 49:10)
Son of Abraham: (Matt. 1:1)
Son of David: (Matt. 9:27; 15:22; 21:9)
Son of the Father: (2 Jn. 1:3)
Son of God: (Mark 1:1; John 9:35; 10:36)
Son of Man: (Matt. 8:20; 9:9; 10:23)
Son of Mary: (Mark 6:3).
Son of the Blessed One (God): (Mark 14:61)
Son of the Highest One (God): (Luke 1:32)
Sower (the): (Matt. 13:37)
Spiritual Rock (that): (1 Cor. 10:4)
Star: (Num. 24:17)
Stone: (Matt. 21:42)
Stone Cut Without Hands: (Dan. 2:34)
Stone of Stumbling: (1 Pet. 2:8)
Stranger unto My Brethren (Ps. 69:8).
Strength and My Song (my): (Isa. 25:4)
Strong Hold (a): (Nahum 1:7)
Strong Rock (my): (Ps. 31:2)
Strong Tower (a): (Ps. 61:3)
Sun of Righteousness: (Mal. 4:2)
Sure Foundation: (Isa. 28:16)
Surety (Guarantee): (Heb. 7:22)
Sweet-smelling Savor (a): (Eph. 5:2)

~T~

Teacher: (John 3:2)
Temple (tabernacle): (1 Kgs. 6:1, 38; John 2:21; Heb. 9:8, 11)
Tender Plant: (Isa. 53:2)
Testator: (Heb. 9:15-17)
Tried (Tested) Stone: (Isa. 28:16)
True God: (1 Jn. 5:20)

Hallowed Be Thy Name

True Vine: (John 15:1)
Truth: (John 14:6)

~U~

Unspeakable Gift: (2 Cor. 9:15)
Upholder of All Things: (Heb. 1:3)

~V~

Veil (His body): (Heb. 10:20)
Very Christ: (Acts 9:22)
Vine (the): (John 15:1)

~W~

Wall of Fire (a): (Zech. 2:5)
Way (the): (John 14:6)
Which is, which was, which is to come: (Rev. 1:4)
Wisdom: (Prov. 8:12)
Wisdom of God (the): (1 Cor. 1:24)
Witness: (Isa. 55:4; Rev. 1:5)
Wonderful: (Isa. 9:6)
Word (the): (John 1:1)
Word of God: (Rev. 19:13)
Word of Life: (1 Jn. 1:1)

~Y~

Young Child (the): (Matt. 2:9)

Appendix B
The Lord's Supper and Table

Often the biblical term "the Lord's Table" (speaking of a spiritual table in which we receive blessing and fellowship in Christ – 1 Corinthians 10) is confused with the biblical term "the Lord's Supper" (the remembrance meeting of the local church spoken of in 1 Corinthians 11). The Lord's Table speaks to the sum total of the spiritual blessings we have in Christ, while the Lord's Supper refers to the remembrance meeting of the Church. In the sense that the souls of believers are refreshed through Spirit-led worship, the Lord's Table probably includes the Lord's Supper, but the distinction of terminology and significance of each should not be lost. The following tables summarize the similarities and differences of the Lord's Table and the Lord's Supper.

Similarities of the Lord's Table and the Lord's Supper
Both speak of bread and a cup
Both are the Lord's (The Lord's Supper doesn't belong to any special group or sect of Christianity.)
Invited by the Lord to participate (We may welcome believers to the Lord's Supper, but cannot invite them.)
Both confer a privilege, but also demand responsibility

Differences	The Lord's Table (1 Cor. 10:16-22)	The Lord's Supper (1 Cor. 11:17-34)
The Term	"Table"	"Supper"
Term Usage	Used in both Old and New Testaments (1 Cor. 9:13; 10:18; Mal. 1:7; 12) In OT, the altar was the Table of the Lord. Priests derived their sustenance by <u>partaking</u> from the altar (Lev. 6:16, 26; 7:6, 31-32; Ezek. 41:22). Other usages where the Table is tied to <u>provision</u> (Ps. 23:5; 78:19). Example: 2 Samuel 9:13 (David/Mephibosheth).	Used only in New Testament (for the Church) Specific: used to describe when Christians gather to <u>remember</u> Christ.
Context of Usage	"communion," "partakers," "fellowship"	"remembering the Lord, proclaiming His death"
Who Gathers	A believer is already there (no steps necessary); it is a personal reality.	*"when you gather together"* (vv.18, 20). It is a corporate reality; an assembly of God's people come together.
Compared to other Tables	Yes, Table of Israel (Mal. 1:12) and Lord's Table (1 Cor. 10:20-21) are compared to the Table of demons.	Not compared with another Table (It is a supper.).
Occurrence of Participation	No mention of "coming together", provisions are continually provided after rebirth (Heb. 4:13-16). Any time – all the time.	*"For as often as ye"* (v. 26). From Acts 20:7, we learn the early church kept the Lord's Supper once a week on Sunday.

Appendix B – The Lord's Supper and Table

Differences	The Lord's Table (1 Cor. 10:16-22)	The Lord's Supper (1 Cor. 11:17-34)
View	Invisible to the world	Visible to the world
Participation	Provision provided as needed and desired.	Commanded by the Lord (an ordinance)
Spread by	God for His people.	God's people for God.
Exclusion from Participation	*"He who comes unto Me I in no way cast out"* (John 6:37). *"Come unto Me, all you that labor and are heavy laden, and I will give you rest"* (Matt. 11:28). God is Sovereign over His Table.	Though the Lord invites all believers to the Lord's Supper, an assembly can exclude those in unconfessed sin (1 Cor. 5:3-5) or holding false doctrine (Titus 3:10, 2 Thess. 3:6, 14) from participating.
Order of Symbols	Cup first – speaks of redemption, the medium first necessary to place one in the body. Bread second – speaks of the communion and fellowship within the body of Christ.	Bread first – speaks of the "physical" body of the Lord being broken for us. Cup second – speaks of the Lord's blood shed for the remission of sins.
Warnings	About "living" unworthily	About "eating" unworthily
Second Coming	No mention – because believers will always receive provisions from Christ.	Observed only until He comes for the Church; we will no longer need a reminder He is coming, since we will have the reality (the Lord).

141

Endnotes

What's in a Name?

1. Howard Clark Kee editor, *Cambridge Annotated Study Bible: Names of God* (Parsons Technology, Inc. Cedar Rapids, IA – electronic copy)
2. Edythe Draper, *Draper's Quotations from the Christian World* (Tyndale House Publishers Inc., Wheaton, IL – electronic copy)
3. Ibid.
4. Merrill F. Unger and William White, Jr., eds., *Nelson's Expository Dictionary of the Old Testament* (Nashville: Nelson, 1980), pp. 228–229
5. P. P. Enns, *The Moody Handbook of Theology* (Moody Press, Chicago, IL; 1989 – electronic copy)
6. P. J. Achtemeier, *Harper's Bible Dictionary* (Harper & Row, P., & Society of Biblical Literature, San Francisco, CA; 1985 – electronic copy)
7. Ibid.
8. Harry A. Ironside, *The Continual Burnt Offering* (Loizeaux Brothers, Neptune, NJ; 1994) January 10th

The Third Commandment

1. Website: http://www.smokeybear.com/vault/history_main.asp
2. W. J. Federer, *Great Quotations: A Collection of Passages, Phrases, and Quotations Influencing Early and Modern World History Referenced according to their Sources in Literature, Memoirs, Letters, Governmental Docs, Speeches, Charters, Court Decisions and Constitutions* (AmeriSearch, St. Louis, MO; 2001)

The Third Commandment (cont.)

3. Ibid.
4. Website: http://www.newswithviews.com/Devvy/kidd94.htm
5. Carol Norris Greene, *Trashing the Name of Jesus Christ* (June 2, 2006) http://www.the-tidings.com/2006/0602/greene.htm
6. Charles Hodge, *Systematic Theology* (Logos Research Systems, Inc., Oak Harbor, WA; 1997 – electronic copy)
7. Ibid.
8. Warren Wiersbe, *Be Holy: An Old Testament Study—Leviticus* (Victor Books, Wheaton, IL; 1994 – electronic copy)

Blasphemy

1. Matthew Henry, *Matthew Henry's Commentary on the Whole Bible* (Hendrickson, Peabody, MA; 1991 – electronic version)
2. William MacDonald, *Believer's Bible Commentary* (Thomas Nelson Publishers, Nashville, TN; 1989), p. 2080
3. Ibid., p. 1251

Causing Others to Blaspheme God

1. Ibid., p. 2095
2. Edythe Draper, op. cit.
3. W. Grinton Berry editor, *Foxe's Book of Martyrs* (Power Books, Old Tappan, NJ; no date), p. 22
4. Charles Spurgeon, *Spurgeon's Morning and Evening Devotions,* (Electronic Edition STEP Files, Parsons Technology, Inc; 1999), Feb. 8 – Morning

Rightly Using the Lord's Name

1. Sir Robert Anderson, *The Honour of His Name* (James Nisbet & Co., London; 1912), chp. 5
2. T. Ernest Wilson, *The Greatness of Christ's Name and Person* (website:http:/www.voicesforChrist.org).
3. Sir Robert Anderson, op. cit., chp. 11
4. Adolf Hitler, *Mein Kampf* (Mariner Books; 1998), vol. 2, chp. 1
5. J. G. Bellett, *The Evangelists, Meditations on the Four Gospels* (Bible Truth Publishers, Addison, IL; no date), p. 4

Rightly Using the Lord's Name (cont.)

6. Sir Robert Anderson, op. cit., chp. 6
7. Ibid., chp. 6
8. Henry M. Morris, *Days of Praise* (Institute for Creation Research, Santee, CA), May 6th

The Lord of Titles

1. Kenneth Wuest, *Word Studies in the Greek New Testament Vol. 3*, (Eerdmans Publishing Co., Grand Rapids, MI; 1973), p. 31
2. August Van Ryn, *Revelation* (Walterick Publishers, Kansas City, KS; no date), p. 35
3. Kenneth S. Wuest, *The New Testament: An Expanded Translation* (Eerdmans Publishing Co., Grand Rapids, MI; 1989), 1 Peter 5:3
4. W. E. Vine, Vine's *Expository Dictionary of Biblical Words* (Thomas Nelson Publishers; 1985 – electronic version), *Kleros*
5. Harry A. Ironside, *Commentary on 1 Peter* (Loizeaux Brothers, Inc., Neptune, NJ; 1985), p. 56
6. J. I. Packer, *Keeping Step with the Spirit* (Fleming H. Revell Co., Old Tappan, NJ; 1984) p. 29
7. Edythe Draper, op. cit.
8. J. H. Thayer, *Thayer's Greek Lexicon* (Biblesoft Electronic Database; 2000), *Nicolaitan*

The Lord of Gatherings

1. Leighton Ford, *The Christian Persuader* (Harper & Row, N.Y.; 1966), p. 49.
2. Kenneth S. Wuest, op. cit., Phil. 1:10
3. *The American Heritage Dictionary* (Houghton Mifflin Company, Boston, MA; 1978)
4. W. E. Vine, op. cit., Worship
5. Kenneth C. Fleming, *He Humbled Himself: Recovering the Lost Art of Serving* (Crossway Books, Wheaton, IL; 1989), pp. 15-16
6. Edythe Draper, op. cit.
7. Website: http://www.withchrist.org/MJS/pbs.htm
8. Website:http://www.wesleyblog.com/evangelism/index.html

The Head – The Lord of Gatherings (cont.)

9. E. Schuyler English, *H. A. Ironside, Ordained of the Lord* (Loizeaux Brothers Inc., Neptune, NJ; 1976). p. 132

The Blessings of the Lord's Name

1. Charles Finney, *The Use and Prevalence of Christ's Name* (from *Lectures on the Conditions of Prevailing Prayer* – Oberlin College; 1850 – copyright by Gospel Truth Ministries), website: http://www.gospeltruth.net
2. John MacArthur, *Alone with God* (Victor Books, Wheaton, IL; 1995 – electronic copy)
3. Matthew Henry, *Commentary on the Whole Bible, vol 6*, (Hendrikson Publishers, Peadbody, MA; 1991), p. 32
4. W. Grinton Berry, op. cit., p. 9
5. *Foxe's Book of Martyrs* (Electronic Edition STEP Files, Parsons Technology, Inc; 1999), chp. 16
6. C. H. Mackintosh, The Mackintosh Treasury (Loizeaux Brothers, Inc., Neptune, NJ 1976; reprint by Believers Bookshelf Inc.; 1999), p. 824
7. Ibid., p. 794
8. Ibid., p. 797
9. Adam Clarke, *Commentary on Psalm 8:1* (Electronic Edition STEP Files, Parsons Technology, Inc; 1999)
10. Warren Wiersbe, *Be Complete: A New Testament Study - Colossians* (Victor Books, Wheaton, Il; 1996 – electronic copy)

I Will Sanctify My Great Name

1. Thomas Brooks, *The Works of Thomas Brooks – Volume 1* (The Banner of Truth Trust, Carlisle, PA; 1980), p. 291
2. Website: http://www.wesleyblog.com/evangelism/index.html
3. Edythe Draper, op. cit.

Bibliography

P. J. Achtemeier, *Harper's Bible Dictionary* (Harper & Row, P., & Society of Biblical Literature, San Francisco, CA; 1985 – electronic copy)

Sir Robert Anderson, *The Honour of His Name* (James Nisbet & Co., London; 1912)

J. G. Bellett, *The Evangelists, Meditations on the Four Gospels* (Bible Truth Publishers, Addison, IL)

David Bercot, *A Dictionary of Early Christian Beliefs* (Hendrickson Publishers, Peabody, MA: 1998)

W. Grinton Berry editor, *Foxe's Book of Martyrs* (Power Books, Old Tappan, NJ; no date)

Thomas Brooks, *The Works of Thomas Brooks – Volume 1* (The Banner of Truth Trust, Carlisle, PA; 1980), p. 291

Trent C. Butler, General Editor, *Holman's Bible Dictionary* (Holman Bible Publisher – Electronic Edition STEP Files, Parsons Technology, Inc; 1999)

Adam Clarke, *Commentary on Acts* (Electronic Edition STEP Files, Parsons Technology, Inc; 1999)

Edythe Draper, *Draper's Quotations from the Christian World* (Tyndale House Publishers Inc., Wheaton, IL – electronic copy)

E. Schuyler English, *H. A. Ironside, Ordained of the Lord* (Loizeaux Brothers Inc., Neptune, NJ; 1976)

P. P. Enns, *The Moody Handbook of Theology* (Moody Press, Chicago, IL; 1989 – electronic copy)

147

W. J. Federer, *Great Quotations: A Collection of Passages, Phrases, and Quotations Influencing Early and Modern World History Referenced according to their Sources in Literature, Memoirs, Letters, Governmental Documents, Speeches, Charters, Court Decisions and Constitutions* (AmeriSearch, St. Louis, MO; 2001)

Charles Finney, *The Use and Prevalence of Christ's Name* (from *Lectures on the Conditions of Prevailing Prayer* – Oberlin College; 1850 – Gospel Truth Ministries) website: http://www.gospeltruth.net

Kenneth C. Fleming, *He Humbled Himself: Recovering the Lost Art of Serving* (Crossway Books, Wheaton, IL; 1989)

Leighton Ford, *The Christian Persuader* (Harper & Row, N.Y.; 1966)

Matthew Henry, *Matthew Henry's Commentary on the Whole Bible* (Hendrickson, Peabody, MA; 1991 – electronic version)

Adolf Hitler, *Mein Kampf* (Mariner Books; reissue edition; 1998)

Charles Hodge, *Systematic Theology* (Logos Research Systems, Inc., Oak Harbor, WA; 1997 – electronic copy)

Harry A. Ironside, *Commentary on 1 Peter* (Loizeaux Brothers, Inc., Neptune, NJ; 1985)

Harry A. Ironside, *The Continual Burnt Offering* (Loizeaux Brothers, Neptune, NJ; 1994)

Howard Clark Kee editor, *Cambridge Annotated Study Bible: Names of God* (Parsons Technology, Inc. Cedar Rapids, IA – electronic copy)

John MacArthur, *Alone with God* (Victor Books, Wheaton, IL; 1995 – electronic copy)

William MacDonald, *Believer's Bible Commentary* (Thomas Nelson Publishers, Nashville, TN; 1989)

C. H. Mackintosh, The Mackintosh Treasury (Loizeaux Brothers, Inc., Neptune, NJ 1976; reprint by Believers Bookshelf Inc.; 1999)

C. H. Mackintosh, *"Thou and Thy House" – The Mackintosh Treasury* (Gute Botschaft, Dillenburg, Germany, originally pub. 1896, reprinted in 1999 Believers Bookshelf)

Henry M. Morris, *Days of Praise* (Institute for Creation Research, Santee, CA)

Notes on the Bible (Francis Asbury Press, Grand Rapids, MI; 1987)

J. I. Packer, *Keeping Step with the Spirit* (Fleming H. Revell Co., Old Tappan, NJ; 1984)

August Van Ryn, *Revelation* (Walterick Publishers, Kansas City, KS; no date)

Charles Spurgeon, *Spurgeon's Morning and Evening Devotions* (Electronic Edition STEP Files, Parsons Technology, Inc; 1999)

J. H. Thayer, *Thayer's Greek Lexicon* (Biblesoft Electronic Database; 2000)

The American Heritage Dictionary (Houghton Mifflin Company, Boston, MA; 1978)

Merrill F. Unger and **William White, Jr.**, eds., *Nelson's Expository Dictionary of the Old Testament* (Nashville: Nelson, 1980)

W. E. Vine, *Vine's Expository Dictionary of Biblical Words* (Thomas Nelson Publishers; 1985 – electronic version)

Warren Wiersbe, *Be Complete: A New Testament Study – Colossians* (Victor Books, Wheaton, Il; 1996 – electronic copy)

Warren Wiersbe, *Be Determined: An Old Testament Study – Nehemiah* (Victor Books, Wheaton, Il; 1996 – electronic copy)

Warren Wiersbe, *Be Dynamic, Be Daring: Acts 9* (Victor Books, Wheaton, Il; 1996 – electronic copy)

Warren Wiersbe, *Be Holy: An Old Testament Study – Leviticus* (Victor Books, Wheaton, IL; 1994 – electronic copy)

Website: http://www.newswithviews.com/Devvy/kidd94.htm

Website: http://www.smokeybear.com/vault/history_main.asp

Website: http://www.wesleyblog.com/evangelism/index.html

Website: http://www.withchrist.org/MJS/pbs.htm

T. Ernest Wilson, *The Greatness of Christ's Name and Person* (website:http:/www.voicesforChrist.org).

Kenneth S. Wuest, *The New Testament: An Expanded Translation* (Eerdmans Publishing Company, Grand Rapids, MI; 1989)

Be Angry and Sin Not

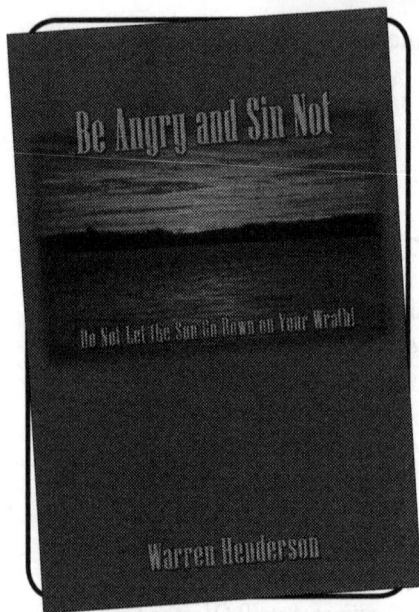

From Scripture, we will learn of God's holy anger, then commence upon the difficult task of aligning our selfish anger and unrighteous behavior with His righteousness. This task will require each of us to honestly evaluate our anger tendencies, to remove internal conditions that frequently induce angry feelings, and to learn techniques to mange our anger in a God-honoring way. If you mismanage anger, this book will guide you into better self-control.

Be Angry And Sin Not tackles such questions as,

- Why am I angry?
- Should I be angry?
- How do I control my angry feelings?
- How can my anger benefit others and serve God?

Binding: **Paper**

Size: **5.5" X 8.0"**

Page Count: **122 pages**

Item #: **B-7051**

ISBN : **1-897117-05-1**

Genre: **Christian Living**

Warren Henderson

An aerospace engineer, who now serves the Lord with his wife Brenda in "full time" ministry. They are commended by Believers Bible Chapel in Rockford, Illinois. Warren is an itinerant Bible teacher and is involved in writing, evangelism, and church planting.

GOSPEL FOLIO PRESS
I WILL PUBLISH THE NAME OF THE LORD

304 Killaly St. West | Port Colborne | ON | L3K 6A6 | Canada | 1 800 952 2382 | E-mail: info@gospelfolio.com | www.gospelfolio.com

BEHOLD THE SAVIOUR

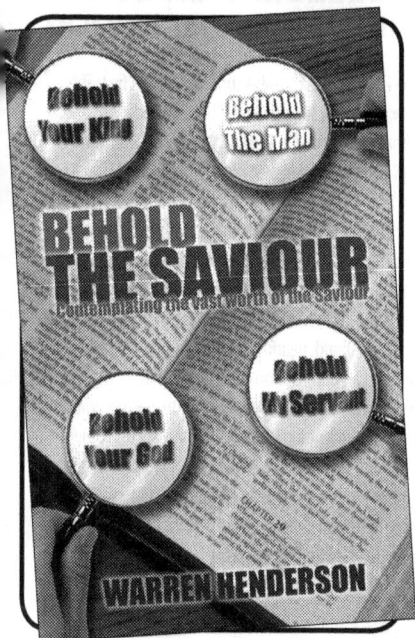

CONTEMPLATING THE VAST WORTH OF THE SAVIOUR

It was refreshing and encouraging to read a book, that did not focus on man's needs or a "how to" method for success. *Behold the Saviour* focuses on the Lord Jesus: His Godhood, human goodness and glories as revealed in the multi-faceted presentation of Holy Scriptures. For when we behold Him in His glory we are *"changed into the same image from glory to glory, even as by the Spirit of the Lord" (2 Cor. 3:18)*.

—Anonymous Pre-Publication Reviewer
(to Christ be the glory!)

Charles Haddon Spurgeon once said, "The more you know **about Christ, the less you will be satisfied with superficial** views of Him." The more we know of Christ, the more we will love and experience Him. This study has refreshed my soul. In the long hours of contemplating the vast worth that the Father attaches to every aspect of the Saviour's life, I have been encouraged to love Him more. If you're feeling a bit dry or spiritually despondent, *Behold the Saviour* afresh – and may the Holy Spirit ignite your passion for Christ and invigorate your ministry for Him.   —Warren Henderson

Binding: **Paper**

Size: **5.5" X 8.5"**

Page Count: **208 pages**

Item #: **B-7272**

ISBN : **1-897117-27-2**

Genre: **Devotional/Commentary**

Warren Henderson

An aerospace engineer, who now serves the Lord with his wife Brenda in "full time" ministry. They are recommended by Believers Bible Chapel in Rockford, Illinois. Warren is an itinerant Bible teacher and is involved in writing, evangelism, and church planting.

GOSPEL FOLIO PRESS
I WILL PUBLISH THE NAME OF THE LORD

304 Killaly St. West | Port Colborne | ON | L3K 6A6 | Canada | 1 800 952 2382 | E-mail: info@gospelfolio.com | www.gospelfolio.com

The Fruitful Vine

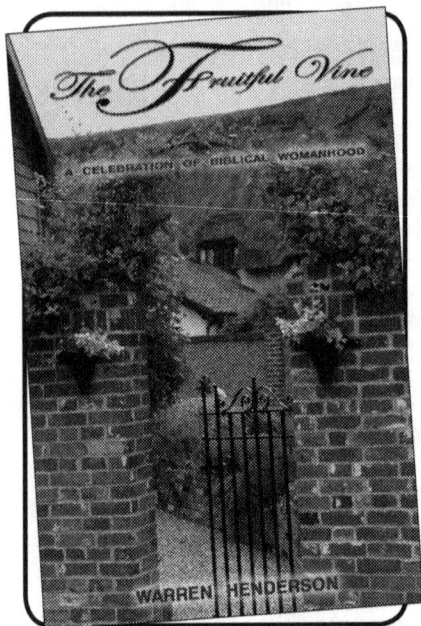

A CELEBRATION OF BIBLICAL WOMANHOOD

The Fruitful Vine contains six sections. The first, The Marital Union, supplies the biblical foundation for the remainder of the book: Why was marriage instituted, and what was God's best plan for marriage? The chapter "To Marry or Not?" offers guidance and encouragement to unmarried women, both those called to "singleness" and those "maids in waiting." The following three sections pertain to the natural roles a married woman will find the most joy in fulfilling - namely, being a companion to her husband, bearing and nurturing children, and keeping an ordered home. The fifth section, The Autumn Years, provides counsel to the "empty-nesters" and encouragement for widows. The final section provides a character sketch of a spiritually-minded woman and the types of ministry she may engage in. Through Scripture, God has revealed both what He finds beautiful in a woman and what He expects of her.

Binding: Paper
Size: 5.5" X 8.0"
Page Count: 172 pages
Item #: B-7132
ISBN : 1-897117-13-2
Genre: Devotional

Warren Henderson
An aerospace engineer, who now serves the Lord with his wife Brenda in "full time" ministry. They are commended by Believers Bible Chapel in Rockford, Illinois. Warren is an itinerant Bible teacher and is involved in writing, evangelism, and church planting.

GOSPEL FOLIO PRESS
I WILL PUBLISH THE NAME OF THE LORD

304 Killaly St. West | Port Colborne | ON | L3K 6A6 | Canada | 1 800 952 2382 | E-mail: info@gospelfolio.com | www.gospelfolio.com

A Genesis
Seeds of Destiny
Devotional

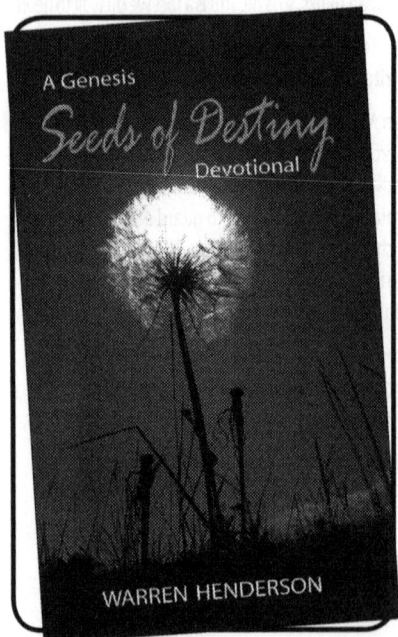

A vast resource of vintage exposition exists from a host of writers who have long since been ushered into the Lord's presence. Most of these books are **out of print and some are diff**icult to obtain.

In general, these writings contain a devotional depth and a Christ-centered attraction that is void in much of today's Christian literature. The author has endeavored to include some of the best gleanings from these writers into this book on Genesis.

Seeds of Destiny is a "commentary style" devotional book which upholds the glories of Christ while exploring Genesis from the whole of Scripture. Warren Henderson presents over 100 brief devotions. This allows the reader to use the book as either a daily devotional or a reference source for deeper study.

Binding: Hard Cover

Size: 6.25" X 9.25"

Page Count: 390 pages

Item #: B-7019

ISBN : 1-897117-01-9

Genre: Devotional

Warren Henderson

An aerospace engineer, who now serves the Lord with his wife Brenda in "full time" ministry. They are commended by Believers Bible Chapel in Rockford, Illinois. Warren is an itinerant Bible teacher and is involved in writing, evangelism, and church planting.

GOSPEL FOLIO PRESS
I WILL PUBLISH THE NAME OF THE LORD

304 Killaly St. West | Port Colborne | ON | L3K 6A6 | Canada | 1 800 952 2382 | E-mail: info@gospelfolio.com | www.gospelfolio.com

www.ingramcontent.com/pod-product-compliance
Lightning Source LLC
Chambersburg PA
CBHW060252050426
42448CB00009B/1626